CLASSIC SERIES

Greatest
Adventure Stories of
Sherlock Holmes

1

V&S PUBLISHERS

Published by:

V&S PUBLISHERS

F-2/16, Ansari road, Daryaganj, New Delhi-110002
☎ 23240026, 23240027 • *Fax:* 011-23240028
Email: info@vspublishers.com • *Website:* www.vspublishers.com

Regional Office : Hyderabad

5-1-707/1, Brij Bhawan (Beside Central Bank of India Lane)
Bank Street, Koti, Hyderabad - 500 095
☎ 040-24737290
E-mail: vspublishershyd@gmail.com

Branch Office : Mumbai

Flat No. Ground Floor, Sonmegh Building
No. 51, Karel Wadi, Thakurdwar, Mumbai - 400 002
☎ 022-22098268
E-mail: vspublishersmum@gmail.com

Follow us on: 🇹 f in

For any assistance sms **VSPUB** to **56161**

All books available at **www.vspublishers.com**

© **Copyright:** V&S PUBLISHERS
ISBN 978-93-505709-9-9
Edition 2014

Printed at : Param Offseters, Okhla, New Delhi-110020

Publisher's Note

It has been our constant endeavour at the **V&S Publishers** to publish all kinds of books ranging from Fiction, Non-fiction, Storybooks, Children Encyclopaedias, to Self-Help, Science Books, Dictionaries, Grammar Books, Self-Development, Management Books, etc.

However, this is for the first time that we are venturing into the vast, rich and fathomless ocean of English Literature and have come up with a set *of ten storybooks called the Greatest Classic Series* authored by some of the greatest and eminent writers of the world. There is a lot to learn from their writing style, selection of plot, development and building of theme and suspense of the story, emphasis and presentation of characters, dialogues, working towards the climax of the story, presenting the climax, and then finally concluding the story.

Each these books are of about 200 pages containing around ten popular stories or more of renowned authors like Oscar Wilde, Ernest William Hornung, Guy de Maupassant, O. Henry, Saki, Washington Irving, Thomas Hardy, Charles Dickens, Jules Verne, Jack London, Mark Twain, Edgar Allen Poe, H.G.Wells, Ambrose Bierce, Amelia Edwards, Edith Wharton, Wilkie Collins and many more. The series is called The Greatest Classic Series as all the names of the books begin with the word, `Greatest' like the Greatest Adventurous Stories, Greatest Detective Stories, Greatest Love Stories, Greatest Ghost Stories, and so on. Besides this, three of the ten books are exclusively on the Adventures of Sherlock Holmes, one of the best detectives the world has ever known written by none other than Sir Arthur Conan Doyle.

Besides the above mentioned characteristics, the books contain an introductory page before each story introducing the author, his brief life history, notable works and literary achievements. Each story has a set of word meanings on each page followed by an exercise meant exclusively aiming the school students to help them grasp the essence of the story easily and quickly.

These books are not only a boon for the school-going students, particularly studying in senior classes from the seventh standard till the twelfth, but are also a treasure trove for all those young and aspiring writers, voracious readers and lovers of English language and literature.

Each of these ten books focus on a theme, such as adventure, love, terror, humour, or supernatural happenings, and are so captivating and real to life that readers may find it difficult to choose from them and so it's better to pick the entire series.

Wishing you all a happy and enjoyable reading...

Contents

Sir Arthur Conan Doyle

Born on May 22, 1859

Died on July 7, 1930

Notable Works: *Stories of Sherlock Holmes, The Lost World, A Study in Scarlet, etc.*

Honours: Knight Bachelor (1902) and Archie Goodwin Award (2005)

Early Life

Sir Arthur Ignatius Conan Doyle, DL (a Deputy Lieutenant is a military commission in the United Kingdom and one of the several deputies to the Lord Lieutenant of a lieutenancy area) was born on May 22, 1859 at 11 Picardy Place, Edinburgh, Scotland. He was a Scottish physician and writer, most noted for his stories about **the detective, Sherlock Holmes**, generally considered a milestone in the field of crime fiction, and for the **adventures of Professor Challenger.** He was a prolific writer, whose other works include science fiction stories, plays, romances, poetry, non-fiction and historical novels.

His father, Charles Altamont Doyle, was an English of Irish descent, and his mother was an Irish. Although he is now referred to as "Conan Doyle", the origin of this compound surname is uncertain. Supported by wealthy uncles, Conan Doyle was sent to the Roman Catholic Jesuit preparatory school, Hodder Place, Stonyhurst, at the age of nine. He then went on to Stonyhurst College until 1875. From 1875 to 1876, he was educated at the Jesuit school Stella Matutina in Feldkirch, Austria. From 1876 to 1881, he studied medicine at the University of Edinburgh, including a period working in the town of Aston (now a district of Birmingham) and in Sheffield, as well as in Shropshire at Ruyton-XI-Towns. Conan Doyle began writing short stories while studying. His earliest extant fiction, "The Haunted Grange of Goresthorpe", was unsuccessfully submitted to Blackwood's Magazine. His first published piece, "The Mystery of Sasassa Valley", a story set in South Africa, was printed in Chambers's Edinburgh Journal on September 6, 1879. Later that month, on September 20, Sir Arthur Conan Doyle published his first non-fictional article, "Gelsemium as a Poison" in the British Medical Journal.

Following his term at the university, he was employed as a doctor on the Greenland whaler - the Hope of Peterhead in 1880 and after his graduation, as a ship's surgeon on the SS Mayumba during a voyage to the West African coast in 1881. He completed his doctorate on the subject of tabes dorsalis in 1885.

Literary Works and Achievements

His practice was initially not very successful. While waiting for patients, Conan Doyle again began writing stories and composed his first novels, *The Mystery of Cloomber*, not published until 1888, and the unfinished *Narrative of John Smith*, which went unpublished until 2011. He amassed a portfolio of short stories including "The Captain of the Pole-Star" and "J. Habakuk Jephson's Statement", both inspired by Doyle's time at sea.

Doyle struggled to find a publisher for his work. His first significant piece, *A Study in Scarlet*, was taken by Ward Lock & Co on November 20, 1886, giving Doyle £25 for all rights to the story. The piece appeared later that year in the Beeton's Christmas Annual and received good reviews in *The Scotsman and the Glasgow Herald*. The story featured the first appearance of Watson and Sherlock Holmes, partially modelled after his former university teacher, Joseph Bell.

Death of Sherlock Holmes

In December 1893, in order to dedicate more of his time to what he considered his more important works (his historical novels), Conan Doyle had Holmes and Professor Moriarty apparently plunge to their deaths together down the Reichenbach Falls in the story "The Final Problem". Public outcry, however, led him to bring the character back in 1901, in "The Hound of the Baskervilles", though this was set at a time before the Reichenbach incident. In 1903, Conan Doyle published his first Holmes short story in ten years, "The Adventure of the Empty House", in which it was explained that only Moriarty had fallen; but since Holmes had other dangerous enemies—especially, Colonel Sebastian Moran—he had arranged to also be perceived as dead. Holmes ultimately was featured in a total of **56 short stories** and **four Conan Doyle novels**, and has since appeared in many novels and stories by other authors too.

Later Years

Following the death of his wife, Louisa in 1906, the death of his son, Kingsley, just before the end of World War I, and the deaths of his brother, Innes, his two brothers-in-laws (one of whom was E. W. Hornung, creator of the literary character, Raffles) and his two nephews, shortly after the war, Conan Doyle sank into depression. He found solace supporting spiritualism and its attempts to find proof of existence beyond the grave. He was also a member of the renowned paranormal organisation, **The Ghost Club**. Its focus, then and now, is on the scientific study of alleged paranormal activities in order to prove (or refute) the existence of paranormal phenomena.

His book, *The Coming of the Fairies (1921)* shows he was apparently convinced of the veracity of the five Cottingley Fairies photographs (which decades later were exposed as a hoax). *In The History of Spiritualism* (1926), Conan Doyle praised the psychic phenomena and spirit materialisations produced by Eusapia Palladino and Mina "Margery" Crandon.

Sir Arthur Conan Doyle was found clutching his chest in the hall of Windlesham, his house in Crowborough, East Sussex, on July 7, 1930. He died of a heart attack at the age of 71. His grave is at Minstead, England.

Trivia

A statue honours Conan Doyle at Crowborough Cross in Crowborough, where he lived for 23 years. There is also a statue of Sherlock Holmes in Picardy Place, Edinburgh, close to the house, where Conan Doyle was born.

The Reigate Puzzle

~Arthur Conan Doyle

IT was some time before the health of my friend Mr. Sherlock Holmes *recovered* from the strain caused by his immense exertions in the spring of '87. The whole question of the Netherland–Sumatra Company and of the colossal schemes of Baron Maupertuis are too recent in the minds of the public, and are too intimately concerned with politics and finance to be fitting subjects for this series of sketches. They led, however, in an indirect fashion to a singular and complex problem which gave my friend an opportunity of demonstrating the value of a fresh weapon among the many with which he waged his life-long battle against crime.

On referring to my notes I see that it was upon the 14th of April that I received a telegram from Lyons which informed me that Holmes was lying ill in Hotel Dulong. Within twenty-four hours I was in his sick room, and was relieved to find that there was nothing formidable in his symptoms. Even his iron constitution, however, had broken down under the *strain* of an investigation which had extended over two months, during which period he had never worked less than fifteen hours a day, and had more than once, as he assured me, kept to his task for five days at a stretch. Even the *triumphant* issue of his labours could not save him from reaction after so terrible an exertion, and at a time when Europe was ringing with his name and when his room was literally ankle-deep with congratulatory telegrams, I found him a *prey* to the blackest depression. Even the knowledge that he had succeeded where the police of three countries had failed, and that he had outmanoeuvred at every point the most accomplished swindler in Europe, was insufficient to rouse him from his nervous prostration.

Three days later we were back in Baker Street together; but it was evident that my friend would be much the better for a change, and the thought of a week of spring time in the country was full of attractions to me also. My old friend, Colonel Hayter, who had come under my professional care in Afghanistan, had now taken a house near Reigate in Surrey, and had frequently asked me to come down to him upon a visit. On the last

Recover – *Get well*
Strain – *Sprain*
Triumphant – *Victorious*
Prey – *Victim*

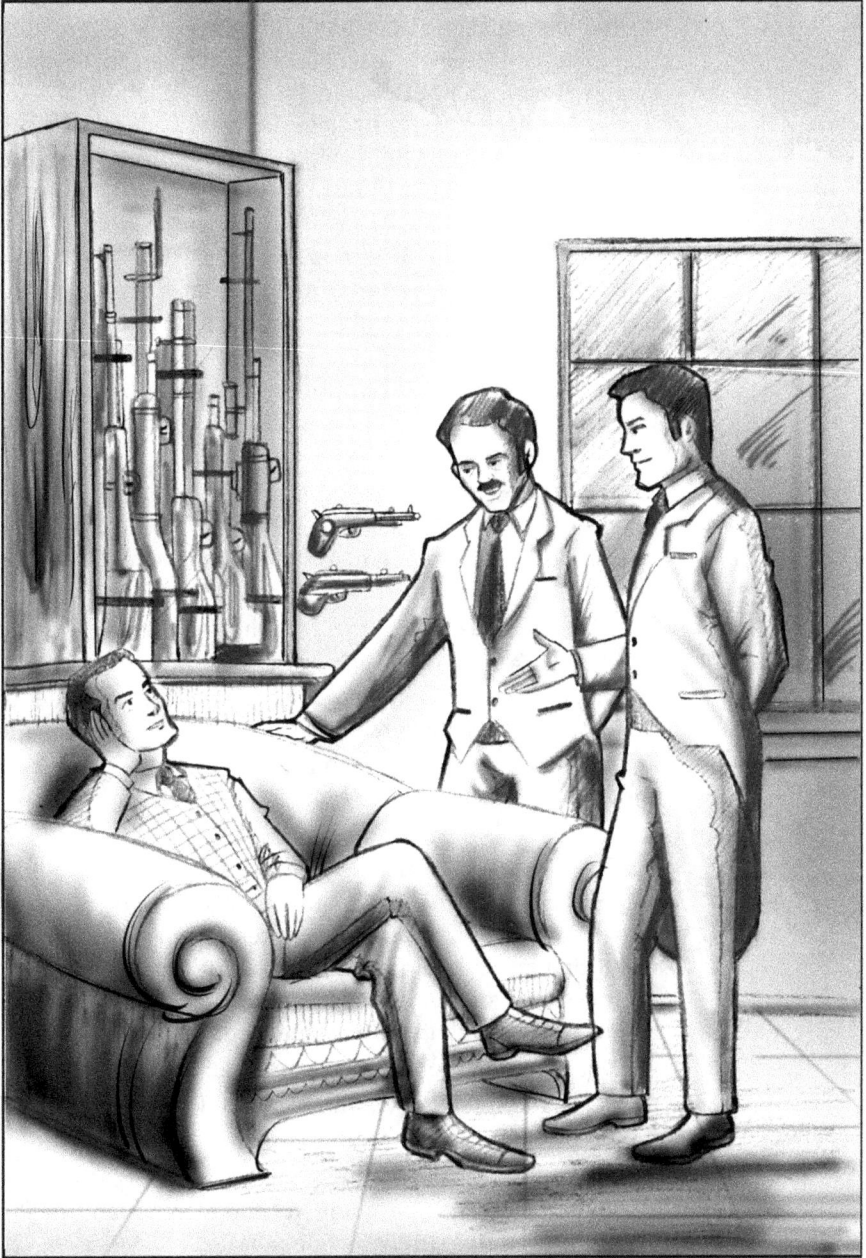

occasion he had remarked that if my friend would only come with me he would be glad to extend his hospitality to him also. A little *diplomacy* was needed, but when Holmes understood that the establishment was a bachelor one, and that he would be allowed the fullest freedom, he fell in with my plans and a week after our return from Lyons, we were under the Colonel's roof. Hayter was a fine old soldier who had seen much of the world, and he soon found, as I had expected, that Holmes and he had much in common.

On the evening of our arrival, we were sitting in the Colonel's gun room after dinner, Holmes stretched upon the sofa, while Hayter and I looked over his little *armory* of Eastern weapons.

"By the way," said he suddenly, "I think I'll take one of these pistols upstairs with me in case we have an alarm."

"An alarm!" said I.

"Yes, we've had a scare in this part lately. Old Acton, who is one of our county magnates, had his house broken into last Monday. No great damage done, but the fellows are still at large."

"No clue?" asked Holmes, cocking his eye at the Colonel.

"None as yet. But the affair is a pretty one, one of our little country crimes, which must seem too small for your attention, Mr. Holmes, after this great international affair."

Holmes waved away the *compliment*, though his smile showed that it had pleased him.

"Was there any feature of interest?"

"I fancy not. The thieves ransacked the library and got very little for their pains. The whole place was turned upside down, drawers burst open, and presses ransacked, with the result that an odd volume of Pope's 'Homer,' two plated candlesticks, an ivory letter-weight, a small oak barometer, and a ball of twine are all that have vanished."

"What an extraordinary assortment!" I exclaimed.

"Oh, the fellows evidently grabbed hold of everything they could get."

Holmes **grunted** from the sofa.

"The county police ought to make something of that," said he; "why, it is surely obvious that --"

But I held up a warning finger.

Diplomacy – *Negotiation, Tact, Skill*
Armory – *Weapon store*
Compliment – *Praise*
Grunt – *To grumble (in discontent)*

"You are here for a rest, my dear fellow. For Heaven's sake don't get started on a new problem when your nerves are all in shreds."

Holmes shrugged his shoulders with a *glance* of comic resignation towards the Colonel, and the talk drifted away into less dangerous channels.

It was destined, however, that all my professional caution should be wasted, for next morning the problem obtruded itself upon us in such a way that it was impossible to ignore it, and our country visit took a turn which neither of us could have *anticipated*. We were at breakfast when the Colonel's butler rushed in with all his propriety shaken out of him.

"Have you heard the news, sir?" he gasped. "At the Cunningham's sir!"

"Burglary!" cried the Colonel, with his coffee cup in mid-air.

"Murder!" The Colonel whistled. "By Jove!" said he. "Who's killed, then? The J.P. or his son?"

"Neither, sir. It was William the coachman. Shot through the heart, sir, and never spoke again."

"Who shot him, then?"

"The burglar, sir. He was off like a shot and got clean away. He'd just broke in at the pantry window when William came on him and met his end in saving his master's property."

"What time?"

"It was last night, sir, somewhere about twelve."

"Ah, then, we'll step over afterwards," said the Colonel, coolly settling down to his breakfast again. "It's a baddish business," he added when the butler had gone; "he's our leading man about here, is old Cunningham, and a very decent fellow too. He'll be cut up over this, for the man has been in his service for years and was a good servant. It's evidently the same villains who broke into Acton's."

"And stole that very singular collection," said Holmes, thoughtfully.

"Precisely." "Hum! It may prove the simplest matter in the world, but all the same at first glance this is just a little *curious*, is it not? A gang of burglars acting in the country might be expected to vary the scene of their operations, and not to crack two cribs in the same district within a few days.

Glance – *Momentary look*
Anticipate – *Expect*
Curious – *Inquisitive*

When you spoke last night of taking **precautions** I remember that it passed through my mind that this was probably the last parish in England to which the thief or thieves would be likely to turn their attention -- which shows that I have still much to learn."

"I fancy it's some local practitioner," said the Colonel. "In that case, of course, Acton's and Cunningham's are just the places he would go for, since they are far the largest about here."

"And richest?"

"Well, they ought to be, but they've had a lawsuit for some years which has sucked the blood out of both of them, I fancy. Old Acton has some claim on half Cunningham's estate, and the lawyers have been at it with both hands."

"If it's a local villain there should not be much difficulty in running him down," said Holmes with a yawn. "All right, Watson, I don't **intend** to **meddle**."

"Inspector Forrester, sir," said the butler, throwing open the door.

The official, a smart, keen-faced young fellow, stepped into the room. "Good morning, Colonel," said he; "I hope I don't **intrude**, but we hear that Mr. Holmes of Baker Street is here."

The Colonel waved his hand towards my friend, and the Inspector bowed.

"We thought that perhaps you would care to step across, Mr. Holmes."

"The fates are against you, Watson," said he, laughing. "We were chatting about the matter when you came in, Inspector. Perhaps you can let us have a few details." As he leaned back in his chair in the familiar attitude, I knew that the case was hopeless.

"We had no clue in the Acton affair. But here we have plenty to go on, and there's no doubt it is the same party in each case. The man was seen."

"Ah!" "Yes, sir. But he was off like a deer after the shot that killed poor William Kirwan was fired. Mr. Cunningham saw him from the bedroom window, and Mr. Alec Cunningham saw him from the back passage. It was quarter to twelve when the alarm broke out. Mr. Cunningham had just got into bed, and Mr. Alec was smoking a pipe in his dressing gown.

Precaution – *Safety measure*
Intend – *Plan*
Meddle – *Interfere*
Intrude – *Infringe*

They both heard William the coachman calling for help, and Mr. Alec ran down to see what was the matter. The back door was open, and as he came to the foot of the stairs he saw two men wrestling together outside. One of them fired a shot, the other dropped, and the murderer rushed across the garden and over the hedge. Mr. Cunningham, looking out of his bedroom, saw the fellow as he gained the road, but lost sight of him at once. Mr. Alec stopped to see if he could help the dying man, and so the villain got clean away. Beyond the fact that he was a middle-sized man and dressed in some dark stuff, we have no personal clue; but we are making energetic *inquiries*, and if he is a stranger we shall soon find him out."

"What was this William doing there? Did he say anything before he died?"

"Not a word. He lives at the lodge with his mother, and as he was a very *faithful* fellow we imagine that he walked up to the house with the intention of seeing that all was right there. Of course this Acton business has put everyone on their guard. The robber must have just burst open the door -- the lock has been forced -- when William came upon him."

"Did William say anything to his mother before going out?"

"She is very old and deaf, and we can get no information from her. The shock has made her half-witted, but I understand that she was never very bright. There is one very important circumstance, however. Look at this!"

He took a small piece of torn paper from a notebook and spread it out upon his knee.

"This was found between the finger and thumb of the dead man. It appears to be a *fragment* torn from a larger sheet. You will observe that the hour mentioned upon it is the very time at which the poor fellow met his fate. You see that his murderer might have torn the rest of the sheet from him or he might have taken this fragment from the murderer. It reads almost as though it were an appointment."

Holmes took up the scrap of paper, a fac-simile of which is here reproduced.

... at quarter to twelve ... learn what ... may ...

"*Presuming* that it is an appointment," continued the Inspector, "it is of course a conceivable theory that this

Inquiry – *Question, Query*
Faithful – *truthful*
Fragment – *A small portion*
Presume – *Assume, Suppose*

William Kirwan -- though he had the *reputation* of being an *honest* man, may have been in league with the thief. He may have met him there, may even have helped him to break in the door, and then they may have fallen out between themselves."

"This writing is of *extraordinary* interest," said Holmes, who had been examining it with intense *concentration*. "These are much deeper waters than I had thought." He sank his head upon his hands, while the Inspector smiled at the effect which his case had had upon the famous London specialist.

"Your last remark," said Holmes, presently, "as to the possibility of there being an understanding between the burglar and the servant, and this being a note of appointment from one to the other, is an ingenious and not entirely impossible supposition. But this writing opens up --" He sank his head into his hands again and remained for some minutes in the deepest thought. When he raised his face again, I was surprised to see that his cheek was tinged with colour, and his eyes as bright as before his illness. He sprang to his feet with all his old energy.

"I'll tell you what," said he, "I should like to have a quiet little glance into the details of this case. There is something in it which fascinates me extremely. If you will *permit* me, Colonel, I will leave my friend Watson and you, and I will step round with the Inspector to test the truth of one or two little fancies of mine. I will be with you again in half an hour."

An hour and half had elapsed before the Inspector returned alone.

"Mr. Holmes is walking up and down in the field outside," said he. "He wants us all four to go up to the house together."

"To Mr. Cunningham's?"

"Yes, sir."

"What for?"

The Inspector shrugged his shoulders. "I don't quite know, sir. Between ourselves, I think Mr. Holmes had not quite got over his illness yet. He's been behaving very queerly, and he is very much excited."

"I don't think you need alarm yourself," said I. "I have usually found that there was method in his madness."

"Some folks might say there was madness in his method," *muttered* the Inspector. "But he's all on fire to start, Colonel, so we had best go out if you are ready."

Reputation – *Status*
Honest – *Truthful*
Extraordinary
– *Uncommon*
Exceptional
Concentration –
Attentiveness
Permit – *Authorize,*
Allow
Mutter – *Talk softly*

We found Holmes pacing up and down in the field, his chin sunk upon his breast, and his hands thrust into his trousers, pockets.

"The matter grows in interest," said he. "Watson, your country trip has been a distinct success. I have had a charming morning."

"You have been up to the scene of the crime, I understand," said the Colonel.

"Yes; the Inspector and I have made quite a little reconnaissance together."

"Any success?"

"Well, we have seen some very interesting things. I'll tell you what we did as we walk. First of all, we saw the body of this **unfortunate** man. He certainly died from a revolver wound as reported." "Had you doubted it, then?"

"Oh, it is as well to test everything. Our inspection was not wasted. We then had an interview with Mr. Cunningham and his son, who were able to point out the exact spot where the murderer had broken through the garden hedge in his flight. That was of great interest."

"Naturally." "Then we had a look at this poor fellow's mother. We could get no information from her, however, as she is very old and **feeble**."

"And what is the result of your investigations?"

"The conviction that the crime is a very **peculiar** one. Perhaps our visit now may do something to make it less **obscure**. I think that we are both agreed, Inspector that the fragment of paper in the dead man's hand, bearing, as it does, the very hour of his death written upon it, is of extreme importance."

"It should give a clue, Mr. Holmes."

"It does give a clue. Whoever wrote that note was the man who brought William Kirwan out of his bed at that hour. But where is the rest of that sheet of paper?"

"I examined the ground carefully in the hope of finding it," said the Inspector.

"It was torn out of the dead man's hand. Why was some one so anxious to get possession of it? Because it incriminated him. And what would he do with it? Thrust it into his pocket, most likely, never noticing that a corner of it had been left in

Unfortunate – *Unlucky*
Feeble – *Weak*
Peculiar – *Strange Queer*
Obscure – *Note Clear, Incomprehensible*

the grip of the corpse. If we could get the rest of that sheet, it is obvious that we should have gone a long way towards solving the mystery."

"Yes, but how can we get at the criminal's pocket before we catch the criminal?"

"Well, well, it was worth thinking over. Then there is another obvious point. The note was sent to William. The man who wrote it could not have taken it; otherwise, of course, he might have delivered his own message by word of mouth. Who brought the note, then? Or did it come through the post?"

"I have made inquiries," said the Inspector. "William received a letter by the afternoon post yesterday. The envelope was destroyed by him."

"Excellent!" cried Holmes, clapping the Inspector on the back. "You've seen the postman. It is a pleasure to work with you. Well, here is the lodge, and if you will come up, Colonel, I will show you the scene of the crime."

We passed the pretty cottage where the murdered man had lived, and walked up an oak-lined *avenue* to the fine old Queen Anne house, which bears the date of Malplaquet upon the *lintel* of the door. Holmes and the Inspector led us around it until we came to the side gate, which is separated by a stretch of garden from the hedge which lines the road. A constable was standing at the kitchen door.

"Throw the door open, officer," said Holmes. "Now, it was on those stairs that young Mr. Cunningham stood and saw the two men struggling just where we are. Old Mr. Cunningham was at that window -- the second on the left -- and he saw the fellow get away just to the left of that bush. Then Mr. Alec ran out and knelt beside the *wounded* man. The ground is very hard, you see, and there are no marks to guide us." As he spoke two men came down the garden path, from around the angle of the house. The one was an elderly man, with a strong, deep-lined, heavy-eyed face; the other a dashing young fellow, whose bright, smiling expression and showy dress were in strange contract with the business which had brought us there.

"Still at it, then?" said he to Holmes. "I thought you Londoners were never at fault. You don't seem to be so very quick, after all."

Avenue – *Path*
Lintel – *Beam*
Wounded – *Injured*

"Ah, you must give us a little time," said Holmes good-humouredly.

"You'll want it," said young Alec Cunningham. "Why, I don't see that we have any clue at all."

"There's only one," answered the Inspector. "We thought that if we could only find -- Good heavens, Mr. Holmes! What is the matter?"

My poor friend's face had suddenly assumed the most *dreadful* expression. His eyes rolled upwards, his features writhed in *agony*, and with a suppressed *groan* he dropped on his face upon the ground. Horrified at the suddenness and *severity* of the attack, we carried him into the kitchen, where he lay back in a large chair, and breathed heavily for some minutes. Finally, with a shamefaced *apology* for his weakness, he rose once more.

"Watson would tell you that I have only just recovered from a severe illness," he explained. "I am *liable* to these sudden nervous attacks."

"Shall I send you home in my trap?" asked old Cunningham.

"Well, since I am here, there is one point on which I should like to feel sure. We can very easily *verify* it."

"What was it?"

"Well, it seems to me that it is just possible that the arrival of this poor fellow William was not before, but after, the entrance of the burglary into the house. You appear to take it for granted that, although the door was forced, the robber never got in."

"I fancy that is quite obvious," said Mr. Cunningham, grave.

"I was smoking in my dressing room."

"Which window is that?"

"The last on the left next my father's."

"Both of your lamps were lit, of course?"

"Undoubtedly." "There are some very singular points here," said Holmes, smiling. "Is it not extraordinary that a burglary -- and a burglar who had had some previous experience -- should deliberately break into a house at a time when he could see from the lights that two of the family were still afoot?"

Dreadful – *Frightful*
Agony – *Anguish*
Groan – *Cry out*
Severity – *Harshness*
Apology – *Request for forgiveness*
Liable – *Accountable*
Verify – *To prove, confirm*

"He must have been a cool hand."

"Well, of course, if the case were not an odd one we should not have been driven to ask you for an explanation," said young Mr. Alec. "But as to your ideas that the man had robbed the house before William tackled him, I think it a most *absurd notion*. Wouldn't we have found the place disarranged, and missed the things which he had taken?"

"It depends on what the things were," said Holmes. "You must remember that we are dealing with a burglar who is a very peculiar fellow, and who appears to work on lines of his own. Look, for example, at the queer lot of things which he took from Acton's -- what was it? -- a ball of string, a letter weight, and I don't know what other odds and ends."

"Well, we are quite in your hands, Mr. Holmes," said old Cunningham. "Anything which you or the Inspector may suggest will most certainly be done."

"In the first place," said Holmes, "I should like you to offer a reward -- coming from yourself, for the officials may take a little time before they would agree upon the sum, and these things cannot be done too promptly. I have jotted down the form here, if you would not mind signing it. Fifty pound was quite enough, I thought."

"I would willingly give five hundred," said the J.P., taking the slip of paper and the pencil which Holmes handed to him. "This is not quite correct, however," he added, glancing over the document.

"I wrote it rather hurriedly."

"You see you begin, 'Whereas, at about a quarter to one on Tuesday morning an attempt was made,' and so on. It was at a quarter to twelve, as a matter of fact."

I was *pained* at the mistake, for I knew how keenly Holmes would feel any slip of the kind. It was his specialty to be *accurate* as to fact, but his recent illness had shaken him, and this one little incident was enough to show me that he was still far from being himself. He was obviously *embarrassed* for an instant, while the Inspector raised his eyebrows, and Alec Cunningham burst into a laugh. The old gentleman corrected the mistake, however, and handed the paper back to Holmes.

"Get it printed as soon as possible," he said; "I think your idea is an excellent one."

Absurd – *Ridiculous*
Notion – *Belief*
Pained – *Injured, Hurt*
Accurate – *Precise*
Embarrass – *Humiliate*

Holmes put the slip of paper carefully away into his pocket book.

"And now," said he, "it really would be a good thing that we should all go over the house together and make certain that this rather *erratic* burglar did not, after all, carry anything away with him."

Before entering, Holmes made an examination of the door which had been forced. It was evident that a chisel or strong knife had been thrust in, and the lock forced back with it. We could see the marks in the wood where it had been pushed in.

"You don't use bars, then?" he asked.

"We have never found it necessary."

"You don't keep a dog?"

"Yes, but he is chained on the other side of the house."

"When do the servants go to bed?"

"About ten."

"I understand that William was usually in bed also at that hour."

"Yes." "It is singular that on this particular night he should have been up. Now, I should be very glad if you would have the kindness to show us over the house, Mr. Cunningham."

A stone-flagged passage, with the kitchens branching away from it, led by a wooden staircase directly to the first floor of the house. It came out upon the landing opposite to a second more *ornamental* stair which came up from the front hall. Out of this landing opened the drawing room and several bedrooms, including those of Mr. Cunningham and his son. Holmes walked slowly, taking keen note of the architecture of the house. I could tell from his expression that he was on a hot scent, and yet I could not in the least imagine in what direction his *inferences* were leading him.

"My good sir," said Mr. Cunningham with some impatience, "this is surely very unnecessary. That is my room at the end of the stairs, and my son's is the one beyond it. I leave it to your judgement whether it was possible for the thief to have come up here without disturbing us."

"You must try around and get on a fresh scent, I fancy," said the son with a rather *malicious* smile.

"Still, I must ask you to humour me a little further. I should like, for example, to see how far the windows of the

Erratic –
Unpredictable, Essentric
Ornamental –
Decorative
Inference –
Conculsion, Deduction
Malicious – *Hateful, Spiteful*

bedrooms command the front. This, I understand is your son's room" -- he pushed open the door --"and that, I *presume*, is the dressing room in which he sat smoking when the alarm was given. Where does the window of that look out to?" He stepped across the bedroom, pushed open the door, and glanced round the other chamber.

"I hope that you are satisfied now?" said Mr. Cunningham, tartly.

"Thank you, I think I have seen all that I wished."

"Then if it is really necessary we can go into my room."

"If it is not too much trouble."

The J. P. shrugged his shoulders, and led the way into his own chamber, which was a plainly furnished and common-place room. As we moved across it in the direction of the window, Holmes fell back until he and I were the last of the group. Near the foot of the bed stood a dish of oranges and a carafe of water. As we passed it Holmes, to my unutter-able *astonish*ment, leaned over in front of me and deliber-ately knocked the whole thing over. The glass smashed into a thousand pieces and the fruit rolled about into every corner of the room.

"You've done it now, Watson," said he, coolly. "A pretty mess you've made of the carpet."

I stooped in some confusion and began to pick up the fruit, understanding for some reason my *companion* desired me to take the blame upon myself. The others did the same, and set the table on its legs again.

"Hullo!" cried the Inspector, "where's he got to?"

Holmes had disappeared.

"Wait here an instant," said young Alec Cunningham. "The fellow is off his head, in my opinion. Come with me, father, and see where he has got to!"

They rushed out of the room, leaving the Inspector, the Colonel, and me staring at each other.

"'Pon my word, I am inclined to agree with Master Alec," said the official. "It may be the effect of this illness, but it seems to me that --"

His words were cut short by a sudden scream of "Help! Help! Murder!" With a thrill I recognised the voice of that of my friend. I rushed madly from the room on to the landing.

Presume – *Assume*
Astonish – *Surprise*
Companion – *Friend*

The cries, which had sunk down into a hoarse, *inarticulate* shouting, came from the room which we had first visited. I dashed in, and on into the dressing room beyond. The two Cunninghams were bending over the prostrate figure of Sherlock Holmes, the younger clutching his throat with both hands, while the elder seemed to be twisting one of his wrists. In an instant, the three of us had torn them away from him, and Holmes *staggered* to his feet, very pale and evidently greatly exhausted.

"Arrest these men, Inspector," he gasped.

"On what charge?"

"That of murdering their coachman, William Kirwan."

The Inspector stared about him in *bewilderment*. "Oh, come now, Mr. Holmes," said he at last, "I'm sure you don't really mean to --"

"Tut, man, look at their faces!" cried Holmes, curtly.

Never certainly have I seen a plainer *confession* of *guilt* upon human countenances. The older man seemed numbed and dazed with a heavy, sullen expression upon his strongly-marked face. The son, on the other hand, had dropped all that *jaunty*, dashing style which had characterised him, and the ferocity of a dangerous wild beast gleamed in his dark eyes and distorted his handsome features. The Inspector said nothing, but, stepping to the door, he blew his whistle. Two of his constables came at the call.

"I have no alternative, Mr. Cunningham," said he. "I trust that this may all prove to be an absurd mistake, but you can see that -- Ah, would you? Drop it!" He struck out with his hand, and a revolver which the younger man was in the act of cocking clattered down upon the floor.

"Keep that," said Holmes, quietly putting his foot upon it; "you will find it useful at the trial. But this is what we really wanted." He held up a little crumpled piece of paper.

"The remainder of the sheet!" cried the Inspector.

"Precisely." "And where was it?"

"Where I was sure it must be. I'll make the whole matter clear to you presently. I think, Colonel, that you and Watson might return now, and I will be with you again in an hour at the furthest. The Inspector and I must have a word with the prisoners, but you will certainly see me back at luncheon time."

Inarticulate – *Mumbling*

Stagger – *To walk, move, or stand unsteadily*

Bewilderment – *Confusion, Astonishment*

Confession – *Admission*

Guilt – *Remorse*

Jaunty – *Jolly, Cheerful*

Sherlock Holmes was as good as his word, for about one o'clock he rejoined us in the Colonel's smoking room. He was accompanied by a little elderly gentleman, who was introduced to me as the Mr. Acton whose house had been the scene of the original burglary.

"I wished Mr. Acton to be present while I demonstrated this small matter to you," said Holmes, "for it is natural that he should take a keen interest in the details. I am afraid, my dear Colonel, that you must regret the hour that you took in such a stormy *petrel* as I am."

"On the contrary," answered the Colonel, warmly, "I consider it the greatest privilege to have been permitted to study your methods of working. I confess that they quite surpass my expectations, and that I am utterly unable to account for your result. I have not yet seen the *vestige* of a clue."

"I am afraid that my explanation may **disillusion** you but it has always been my habit to hide none of my methods, either from my friend Watson or from any one who might take an intelligent interest in them. But, first, as I am rather shaken by the knocking about which I had in the dressing room, I think that I shall help myself to a dash of your brandy, Colonel. My strength had been rather tried of late."

"I trust that you had no more of those nervous attacks."

Sherlock Holmes laughed heartily. "We will come to that in its turn," said he. "I will lay an account of the case before you in its due order, showing you the various points which guided me in my decision. Pray interrupt me if there is any inference which is not perfectly clear to you.

"It is of the highest importance in the art of detection to be able to recognise, out of a number of facts, which are incidental and which vital. Otherwise your energy and attention must be **dissipated** instead of being concentrated. Now, in this case, there was not the slightest doubt in my mind from the first that the key of the whole matter must be looked for in the scrap of paper in the dead man's hand.

"Before going into this, I would draw your attention to the fact that, if Alec Cunningham's narrative was correct, and if the assailant, after shooting William Kirwan, had instantly fled, then it obviously could not be he who tore

Petrel – *Numerous tube-nosed seabiorls*
Vestige – *Trace, A mark*
Disillusion – *Disenchant*
Dissipate – *Disperse, Dispel*

the paper from the dead man's hand. But if it was not he, it must have been Alec Cunningham himself, for by the time that the old man had *descended*, several servants were upon the scene. The point is a simple one, but the Inspector had overlooked it because he had started with the supposition that these county magnates had had nothing to do with the matter. Now, I make a point of never having any prejudices, and of following docilely wherever fact may lead me, and so, in the very first stage of the investigation, I found myself looking a little *askance* at the part which had been played by Mr. Alec Cunningham.

"And now I made a very careful examination of the corner of paper which the Inspector had submitted to us. It was at once clear to me that it formed part of a very remarkable document. Here it is. Do you not now observe something very suggestive about it?"

"It has a very irregular look," said the Colonel.

"My dear sir," cried Holmes, "there cannot be the least doubt in the world that it has been written by two persons doing alternate words. When I draw your attention to the strong t's of 'at' and 'to', and ask you to compare them with the weak ones of 'quarter' and 'twelve,' you will instantly recognise the fact. A very brief analysis of these four words would enable you to say with the utmost confidence that the 'learn' and the 'maybe' are written in the stronger hand, and the 'what' in the weaker."

"By Jove, it's as clear as day!" cried the Colonel. "Why on earth should two men write a letter in such a fashion?"

"Obviously the business was a bad one, and one of the men who distrusted the other was determined that, whatever was done, each should have an equal hand in it. Now, of the two men, it is clear that the one who wrote the 'at' and 'to' was the ringleader."

"How do you get at that?"

"We might deduce it from the mere character of the one hand as compared with the other. But we have more assured reasons than that for supposing it. If you examine this scrap with attention you will come to the conclusion that the man with the stronger hand wrote all his words first,

Descend – *Go down*
Askance –
Doubtfully, Mistrust
Sufficient – *Enough*

leaving blanks for the other to fill up. These blanks were not always **sufficient**, and you can see that the second man had a squeeze to fit his 'quarter' in between the 'at' and the 'to,' showing that the latter were already written. The man who wrote all his words first in undoubtedly the man who planned the affair."

"Excellent!" cried Mr. Acton.

"But very **superficial**," said Holmes. "We come now, however, to a point which is of importance. You may not be aware that the deduction of a man's age from his writing is one which has brought to considerable **accuracy** by experts. In normal cases, one can place a man in his true decade with tolerable confidence.

I say normal cases, because ill-health and physical weakness reproduce the signs of old age, even when the invalid is a youth. In this case, looking at the bold, strong hand of the one, and the rather broken-backed appearance of the other, which still retains its legibility although the t's have begun to lose their crossing, we can say that the one was a young man and the other was advanced in years without being positively **decrepit**."

"Excellent!" cried Mr. Acton again.

"There is a further point, however, which is **subtler** and of greater interest. There is something in common between these hands. They belong to men who are blood-relatives. It may be most obvious to you in the Greek e's, but to me there are many small points which indicate the same thing. I have no doubt at all that a family mannerism can be traced in these two specimens of writing.

I am only, of course, giving you the leading results now of my examination of the paper. There were twenty-three other deductions which would be of more interest to experts than to you. They all tend to deepen the impression upon my mind that the Cunninghams, father and son, had written this letter.

"Having got so far, my next step was, of course, to examine into the details of the crime, and to see how far they would help us. I went up to the house with the Inspector, and saw all that was to be seen. The wound upon the dead man

Superficial –
Apparent
Accuracy – *Precision*
Subtle – *Slight*
Decrepit - *Made weak by age*

was, as I was able to determine with absolute confidence, fired from a revolver at the distance of something over four yards.

There was no powder-blackening on the clothes. Evidently, therefore, Alec Cunningham had lied when he said that the two men were struggling when the shot was fired. Again, both father and son agreed as to the place where the man escaped into the road. At that point, however, as it happens, there is a broadish ditch, moist at the bottom. As there were no indications of bootmarks about this ditch, I was absolutely sure not only that the Cunninghams had again lied, but that there had never been any unknown man upon the scene at all.

"And now I have to consider the motive of this singular crime. To get at this, I *endeavoured* first of all to solve the reason of the original burglary at Mr. Acton's. I understood, from something which the Colonel told us, that a *lawsuit* had been going on between you, Mr. Acton, and the Cunninghams. Of course, it instantly occurred to me that they had broken into your library with the intention of getting at some document which might be of importance in the case."

"Precisely so," said Mr. Acton. "There can be no possible doubt as to their intentions. I have the clearest claim upon half of their present estate, and if they could have found a single paper -- which, fortunately, was in the strong-box of my solicitors -- they would undoubtedly have crippled our case."

"There you are," said Holmes, smiling. "It was a dangerous, *reckless* attempt, in which I seem to trace the influence of young Alec. Having found nothing they tried to divert suspicion by making it appear to be an ordinary burglary, to which end they carried off whatever they could lay their hands upon.

That is all clear enough, but there was much that was still *obscure*. What I wanted above all was to get the missing part of that note. I was certain that Alec had torn it out of the dead man's hand, and almost certain that he must have *thrust* it into the pocket of his dressing gown. Where else could he have put it? The only question was whether it was still there. It was worth an effort to find out, and for that object we all went up to the house.

Endeavour – *Attempt*
Lawsuit – *Court case*
Reckless – *Irresponsible*
Obscure – *Vague, Incomprehensible*
Thrust – *Push*
Sympathy – *Empathy*
Imposture – *Fraud, Deception*

"The Cunninghams joined us, as you doubtless remember, outside the kitchen door. It was, of course, of the very first importance that they should not be reminded of the existence of this paper, otherwise they would naturally destroy it without delay. The Inspector was about to tell them the importance which we attached to it when, by the luckiest chance in the world, I tumbled down in a sort of fit and so changed the conversation.

"Good heavens!" cried the Colonel, laughing, "do you mean to say all our *sympathy* was wasted and your fit an *imposture*?"

"Speaking professionally, it was admirably done," cried I, looking in amazement at this man who was forever *confounding* me with some new phase of his *astuteness*.

"It is an art which is often useful," said he. "When I recovered I managed, by a device which had perhaps some little merit of ingenuity, to get old Cunningham to write the word 'twelve,' so that I might compare it with the 'twelve' upon the paper."

"Oh, what an ass I have been!" I exclaimed.

"I could see that you were *commiserating* me over my weakness," said Holmes, laughing. "I was sorry to cause you the sympathetic pain which I know that you felt. We then went upstairs together, and having entered the room and seen the dressing gown hanging up behind the door, I contrived, by upsetting a table, to engage their attention for the moment, and slipped back to examine the pockets.

I had hardly got the paper, however -- which was, as I had expected, in one of them -- when the two Cunninghams were on me, and would, I verily believe, have murdered me then and there but for your *prompt* and friendly aid.

As it is, I feel that young man's grip on my throat now, and the father has twisted my wrist round in the effort to get the paper out of my hand. They saw that I must know all about it, you see, and the sudden change from absolute security to complete *despair* made them perfectly desperate.

"I had a little talk with old Cunningham afterwards as to the motive of the crime. He was tractable enough, though his

Decoyed - *A person trapped or tricked*
Confound – *Stun*
Astute – *Shrewd*
Commiserate – *Sympathise*
Prompt – *Punctual, Immediate*
Despair – *Misery*
Levy – *Tax*
Plausible – *Reasonable*

son was a perfect demon, ready to blow out his own or anybody else's brains if he could have got to his revolver. When Cunningham saw that the case against him was so strong he lost all heart and made a clean breast of everything.

It seems that William had secretly followed his two masters on the night when they made their raid upon Mr. Acton's, and having thus got them into his power, proceeded, under threats of exposure, to *levy* blackmail upon them. Mr. Alec, however, was a dangerous man to play games of that sort with.

It was a stroke of positive genius on his part to see in the burglary scare which was convulsing the countryside an opportunity of *plausibly* getting rid of the man whom he feared. William was *decoyed* up and shot, and had they only got the whole of the note and paid a little more attention to detail in the accessories, it is very possible that *suspicion* might never have been aroused."

"And the note?" I asked.

Sherlock Holmes placed the subjoined paper before us.

If you will only come around . . . to the east gate, you will . . . will very much surprise you and . . . be of the greatest service to you and also to Annie Morrison. But say nothing to anyone upon the matter.

"It is very much the sort of thing that I expected," said he. "Of course, we do not yet know what the relations may have been between Alec Cunningham, William Kirwan, and Annie Morrison.

The results show that the trap was skilfully *baited*. I am sure that you cannot fail to be delighted with the traces of heredity shown in the p's and in the tails of the g's. The absence of the i-dots in the old man's writing is also most characteristic. Watson, I think our quiet rest in the country has been a distinct success, and I shall certainly return much *invigorated* to Baker Street tomorrow."

Suspicion – *Doubt*
Baited – *Lured*
Invigorate – *Refresh, Vitalise*

Food For Thought

If Sherlock Holmes would not have found the small piece of torn paper in the dead man's hand, could he be able to solve the case and nab the murderer? If yes, then how, and also explain what were the other clues that could have helped Holmes to catch the culprit?

An Understanding

Q. 1. "I have usually found that there was a method in his madness."
Who spoke these words to whom? About whose madness is the speaker
refering to and what was the method hidden in the madness?

Ans. _____

_____

_____

_____

_____

Q. 2. Why did Sherlock Holmes cry out, "Excellent" and clapped the
Inspector on the back?
Ans. _____

_____

_____

_____

Q. 3. "Good heavens!" cried the Colonel, laughing, "Do you men to say
all our sympahty was wasted and your fit an imposture?" Why did the
Colonel utter these words and on what pretext?
Ans. _____

_____

_____

_____

Q. 4. Why did the two Cunninghams attack Sherlock Holmes and try to
kill him?
Ans. _____

_____

_____

_____

The Red-Headed League
~Arthur Conan Doyle

I had called upon my friend, Mr. Sherlock Holmes, one day in the autumn of last year, and found him in deep conversation with a very **stout**, florid-faced elderly gentleman, with fiery red hair. With an apology for my **intrusion**, I was about to withdraw, when Holmes pulled me abruptly into the room and closed the door behind me.

"You could not possibly have come at a better time, my dear Watson," he said, cordially.

"I was afraid that you were engaged."

"So I am. Very much so."

"Then I can wait in the next room."

"Not at all. This gentleman, Mr. Wilson, has been my partner and helper in many of my most successful cases, and I have no doubt that he will be of the utmost use to me in yours also."

The stout gentleman half rose from his chair and gave a bob of greeting, with a quick little questioning glance from his small, fat-encircled eyes.

"Try the settee," said Holmes, relapsing into his armchair, and putting his finger tips together, as was his custom when in judicial moods. "I know, my dear Watson, that you share my love of all that is **bizarre** and outside the conventions and **humdrum** routine of everyday life. You have shown your relish for it by the enthusiasm which has prompted you to chronicle, and, if you will excuse my saying so, somewhat to **embellish** so many of my own little adventures."

"Your cases have indeed been of the greatest interest to me," I observed.

"You will remember that I remarked the other day, just before we went into the very simple problem presented by Miss Mary Sutherland, that for strange effects and extraordinary combinations we must go to life itself, which is always far more daring than any effort of the imagination." "A proposition which I took the liberty of doubting."

"You did, doctor, but nonetheless, you must come around to my view, for otherwise I shall keep on piling fact upon

Embellish - *Improve a story/statement*
Stout – *Chubby*
Intrusion – *Interruption*
Bizarre – *Strange*
Humdrum – *Dull*

fact on you, until your reason breaks down under them and acknowledge me to be right. Now, Mr. Jabez Wilson here has been good enough to call upon me this morning, and to begin a narrative which promises to be one of the most singular which I have listened to for some time. You have heard me remark that the strangest and most *unique* things are very often connected not with the larger but with the smaller crimes, and occasionally, indeed, where there is room for doubt whether any positive crime has been committed. As far as I have heard, it is impossible for me to say whether the present case is an instance of crime or not, but the course of events is certainly among the most singular that I have ever listened to. Perhaps, Mr. Wilson, you would have the great kindness to *recommence* your narrative. I ask you, not merely because my friend, Dr. Watson, has not heard the opening part, but also because the *peculiar* nature of the story makes me anxious to have every possible detail from your lips. As a rule, when I have heard some slight indication of the course of events, I am able to guide myself by the thousands of other similar cases which occur to my memory. In the present instance. I am forced to admit that the facts are, to the best of my belief, unique."

The *portly* client puffed out his chest with an appearance of some little *pride*, and pulled a dirty and wrinkled newspaper from the inside pocket of his great coat. As he glanced down the advertisement column, with his head thrust forward, and the paper flattened out upon his knee, I took a good look at the man, and *endeavoured*, after the fashion of my companion, to read the indications which might be presented by his dress or appearance.

I did not gain very much, however, by my inspection. Our visitor bore every mark of being an average commonplace British tradesman, *obese*, *pompous*, and slow. He wore rather baggy grey shepherd's check trousers, a not overclean black frock coat, unbuttoned in the front, and a drab waistcoat with a heavy brassy Albert chain, and a square pierced bit of metal dangling down as an ornament. A frayed top hat and a faded brown overcoat with a wrinkled velvet collar lay upon a chair beside him. Altogether, look as I would, there was nothing remarkable about the man save his blazing red head and the expression of extreme *chagrin* and discontent upon his features.

Unique – *Exclusive*
Recommence – *Resume*
Peculiar – *Unusual*
Portly – *Well-built*
Pride – *Arrogance*
Endeavour – *Attempt*
Obese – *Overweight*
Pompous – *Arrogant*
Chagrin – *Mortification*

Sherlock Holmes's quick eye took in my occupation, and he shook his head with a smile as he noticed my questioning *glances*. "Beyond the obvious facts that he has at some time done manual labour, that he takes snuff, that he is a Freemason, that he has been in China, and that he has done a considerable amount of writing lately, I can deduce nothing else."

Mr. Jabez Wilson started up in his chair, with his forefinger upon the paper, but his eyes upon my *companion*.

How, in the name of good fortune, did you know all that, Mr. Holmes?" he asked. "How did you know, for example, that I did manual labour? It's as true as gospel, for I began as a ship's carpenter." "Your hands, my dear sir. Your right hand is quite a size larger than your left. You have worked with it and the muscles are more developed."

"Well, the snuff, then, and the Freemasonry?"

"I won't insult your intelligence by telling you how I read that, especially as, rather against the strict rules of your order, you use an arc and compass breastpin."

"Ah, of course, I forgot that. But the writing?"

"What else can be indicated by that right cuff so very shiny for five inches, and the left one with the smooth patch near the elbow where you rest it upon the desk."

"Well, but China?"

"The fish which you have tattooed immediately above your wrist could only have been done in China. I have made a small study of tattoo marks, and have even contributed to the literature of the subject. That trick of staining the fishes' scales of a delicate pink is quite peculiar to China. When, in addition, I see a Chinese coin hanging from your watch chain, the matter becomes even more simple."

Mr. Jabez Wilson laughed heavily. "Well, I never!" said he. "I thought at first that you had done something clever, but I see that there was nothing in it after all."

"I begin to think, Watson," said Holmes, "that I make a mistake in explaining. 'Omne ignotom pro magnifico,' you know, and my poor little reputation, such as it is, will suffer shipwreck if I am so *candid*. Can you not find the advertisement, Mr. Wilson?"

"Yes, I have got it now," he answered, with his thick, red finger planted halfway down the column. "Here it is. This is what began it all. You just read it for yourself, sir."

Glance – *Glimpse*
Companion – *Friend*
Candid – *Honest*

I took the paper from him and read as follows:

"TO THE RED-HEADED LEAGUE: On account of the *bequest* of the late Ezekiah Hopkins, of Lebanon, Pa., U. S. A., there is now another vacancy open which entitles a member of the League to a salary of four pounds a week for purely nominal services. All red-headed men who are sound in body and mind and above the age of twenty-one years are *eligible*. Apply in person on Monday, at eleven o'clock, to Duncan Ross, at the offices of the League, 7 Pope's Court, Fleet Street."

"What on earth does this mean?" I ejaculated, after I had twice read over the extraordinary announcement. Holmes *chuckled* and wriggled in his chair, as was his habit when in high spirits. "It is a little off the beaten track, isn't it?" said he. "And now, Mr. Wilson, off you go at scratch, and tell us all about yourself, your household, and the effect which this advertisement had upon your fortunes. You will first make a note, doctor, of the paper and the date."

"It is The Morning Chronicle of April 27, 1890. Just two months ago."

"Very good. Now, Mr. Wilson."

"Well, it is just as I have been telling you, Mr. Sherlock Holmes," said Jabez Wilson, *mopping* his forehead, "I have a small pawnbroker's business at Saxe-Coburg Square, near the City. It's not a very large affair, and of late years, it has not done more than just give me a living. I used to be able to keep two assistants, but now I only keep one; and I would have a job to pay him but that he is willing to come for half wages, so as to learn the business."

"What is the name of this obliging youth?" asked Sherlock Holmes.

"His name is Vincent Spaulding, and he's not such a youth either. It's hard to say his age. I should not wish a smarter assistant, Mr. Holmes; and I know very well that he could better himself, and earn twice what I am able to give him. But, after all, if he is satisfied, why should I put ideas in his head?"

"Why, indeed? You seem most fortunate in having an employee who comes under the full market price. It is not a common experience among employers in this age. I don't know that your assistant is not as remarkable as your advertisement."

Bequest –
Inheritance
Eligible – *Entitled*
Chuckle – *Giggle*
Mopping – *Washing*

"Oh, he has his faults, too," said Mr. Wilson. "Never was such a fellow for photography. Snapping away with a camera when he ought to be improving his mind, and then diving down into the *cellar* like a rabbit into its hole to develop his pictures. That is his main fault; but, on the whole, he's a good worker. There's no *vice* in him."

"He is still with you, I *presume*?"

"Yes, sir. He and a girl of fourteen, who does a bit of simple cooking, and keeps the place clean - that's all I have in the house, for I am a widower, and never had any family. We live very quietly, sir, the three of us; and we keep a roof over our heads, and pay our *debts*, if we do nothing more.

"The first thing that put us out was that advertisement. Spaulding, he came down into the office just this day eight weeks, with this very paper in his hand, and he says:

"'I wish to the Lord, Mr. Wilson, that I was a redheaded man.'

"'Why that?' I asks.

"'Why,' says he, 'here's another vacancy on the League of the Red-headed Men. It's worth quite a little fortune to any man who gets it, and I understand that there are more vacancies than there are men, so that the trustees are at their wits' end what to do with the money. If my hair would only change colour, here's a nice little crib all ready for me to step into.'

"'Why, what is it, then?' I asked. You see, Mr. Holmes, I am a very stay-at-home man, and, as my business came to me instead of my having to go to it, I was often weeks on end without putting my foot over the door mat. In that way I didn't know much of what was going on outside, and I was always glad of a bit of news.

"'Have you never heard of the League of the Red-headed Men?' he asked, with his eyes open.

"'Never.' "'Why, I wonder at that, for you are eligible yourself for one of the vacancies.'

"'And what are they worth?' I asked.

"'Oh, merely a couple of hundred a year, but the work is slight, and it need not interfere very much with one's other occupations.'

"Well, you can easily think that that made me prick up my ears, for the business has not been over good for some years, and an extra couple of hundreds would have been very handy.

Cellar – *Vault*
Vice – *Associate*
Presume – *Assume*
Debt – *Arrears*

"'Tell me all about it,' said I.

"'Well,' said he, showing me the advertisement, 'you can see for yourself that the League has a vacancy, and there is the address where you should apply for particulars. As far as I can make out, the League was founded by an American millionaire, Ezekiah Hopkins, who was very *peculiar* in his ways. He was himself red-headed, and had a great sympathy for all red-headed men; so, when he died, it was found that he had left his *enormous fortune* in the hands of trustees, with instructions to apply the interest to the providing of easy berths to men whose hair is of that colour. From all I hear it is splendid pay, and very little to do.'

"'But,' said I, 'there would be millions of red-headed men who would apply.'

"'Not so many as you might think,' he answered. 'You see it is really confined to Londoners, and to grown men. This American had started from London when he was young, and he wanted to do the old town a good turn. Then, again, I have heard it is of no use your applying if your hair is light red, or dark red, or anything but real, bright, blazing, fiery red. Now, if you cared to apply, Mr. Wilson, you would just walk in; but perhaps it would hardly be worth your while to put yourself out of the way for the sake of a few hundred pounds.'

"Now it is a fact, gentlemen, as you may see for yourselves, that my hair is of a very full and rich tint, so that it seemed to me that, if there was to be any competition in the matter, I stood as good a chance as any man that I had ever met. Vincent Spaulding seemed to know so much about it that I thought he might prove useful, so I just ordered him to put up the shutters for the day, and to come right away with me. He was very willing to have a holiday, so we shut the business up, and started off for the address that was given us in the advertisement.

"I never hope to see such a sight as that again, Mr. Holmes. From north, south, east, and west every man who had a shade of red in his hair had tramped into the City to answer the advertisement. Fleet Street was choked with red-headed folk, and Pope's Court looked like a coster's orange barrow. I should not have thought there were so many in the whole country as were brought together by that single advertisement. Every shade of colour they were - straw, lemon, orange, brick, Irish

Peculiar – *Strange*
Enormous –
Massive
Fortune – *Luck*

setter, liver, clay; but, as Spaulding said, there were not many who had the real vivid flame-coloured tint. When I saw how many were waiting, I would have given it up in *despair*; but Spaulding would not hear of it. How he did it I could not imagine, but he pushed and pulled and butted until he got me through the crowd, and right up to the steps which led to the office. There was a double stream upon the stair, some going up in hope, and some coming back *dejected*; but we wedged in as well as we could, and soon found ourselves in the office."

"Your experience has been a most entertaining one," remarked Holmes, as his client paused and refreshed his memory with a huge pinch of snuff. "Pray continue your very interesting statement." "There was nothing in the office but a couple of wooden chairs and a deal table, behind which sat a small man, with a head that was even redder than mine. He said a few words to each candidate as he came up, and then he always managed to find some fault in them which would *disqualify* them. Getting a vacancy did not seem to be such a very easy matter after all. However, when our turn came, the little man was much more favourable to me than to any of the others, and he closed the door as we entered, so that he might have a private word with us.

"'This is Mr. Jabez Wilson,' said my assistant, 'and he is willing to fill a vacancy in the League.'

"'And he is admirably suited for it,' the other answered. 'He has every requirement. I cannot recall when I have seen anything so fine.' He took a step backward, cocked his head on one side, and *gazed* at my hair until I felt quite *bashful*. Then suddenly he plunged forward, wrung my hand, and congratulated me warmly on my success.

"'It would be injustice to hesitate,' said he. 'You will, how-ever, I am sure, excuse me for taking an obvious precaution.' With that he seized my hair in both his hands, and tugged until I yelled with the pain. 'There is water in your eyes,' said he, as he released me. '*I perceive* that all is as it should be. But we have to be careful, for we have twice been deceived by wigs and once by paint. I could tell you tales of cobbler's wax which would disgust you with human nature.' He stepped over to the window and shouted through it at the top of his voice that the vacancy was filled. A *groan* of disappointment came up from below, and the folk all trooped away in different

Despair – *Hopelessness*
Deject – *Discourage*
Disqualify – *Prohibit*
Gaze – *Stare*
Bashful – *Timid*
Perceive – *Distinguish*
Groan – *Moan*

directions, until there was not a red head to be seen except my own and that of the manager.

"'My name,' said he, 'is Mr. Duncan Ross, and I am myself one of the pensioners upon the fund left by our *noble* benefactor. Are you a married man, Mr. Wilson? Have you a family?'

"I answered that I had not.

"His face fell immediately.

"'Dear me!' he said, gravely, 'that is very serious indeed! I am sorry to hear you say that. The fund was, of course, for the *propagation* and spread of the red heads as well as for their maintenance. It is exceedingly unfortunate that you should be a bachelor.'

"My face lengthened at this, Mr. Holmes, for I thought that I was not to have the vacancy after all; but, after thinking it over for a few minutes, he said that it would be all right.

"'In the case of another,' said he, 'the objection might be fatal, but we must stretch a point in favour of a man with such a head of hair as yours. When shall you be able to enter upon your new duties?'

"'Well, it is a little awkward, for I have a business already,' said I.

"'Oh, never mind about that, Mr. Wilson!' said Vincent Spaulding. 'I shall be able to look after that for you.'

"'What would be the hours?' I asked.

"'Ten to two.'

"Now a pawnbroker's business is mostly done of an evening, Mr. Holmes, especially Thursday and Friday evenings, which is just before pay day; so it would suit me very well to earn a little in the mornings. Besides, I knew that my assistant was a good man, and that he would see to anything that turned up.

"'That would suit me very well,' said I. 'And the pay?'

"'Is four pounds a week.'

"'And the work?'

"'Is purely *nominal*.'

"'What do you call purely nominal?'

"'Well, you have to be in the office, or at least in the building, the whole time. If you leave, you forfeit your whole position forever. The will is very clear upon that point. You don't

Noble – *Dignified*
Propagation –
Spread
Nominal – *Minimal*

comply with the conditions if you budge from the office during that time.'

"'It's only four hours a day, and I should not think of leaving,' said I.

"'No excuse will avail,' said Mr. Duncan Ross, 'neither sickness, nor business, nor anything else. There you must stay, or you lose your billet.'

"'And the work?'

"'Is to copy out the "Encyclopaedia Britannica." There is the first volume of it in that press. You must find your own ink, pens, and blotting paper, but we provide this table and chair. Will you be ready tomorrow?'

"'Certainly,' I answered.

"'Then, goodbye, Mr. Jabez Wilson, and let me congratulate you once more on the important position which you have been *fortunate* enough to gain.' He bowed me out of the room, and I went home with my assistant hardly knowing what to say or do, I was so pleased at my own good fortune.

"Well, I thought over the matter all day, and by evening, I was in low spirits again; for I had quite *persuaded* myself that the whole affair must be some great *hoax* or fraud, though what its object might be I could not imagine. It seemed altogether past belief that anyone could make such a will, or that they would pay such a sum for doing anything so simple as copying out the 'Encyclopaedia Britannica.' Vincent Spaulding did what he could to cheer me up, but by bedtime, I had reasoned myself out of the whole thing. However, in the morning, I determined to have a look at it anyhow, so I bought a penny bottle of ink, and with a quill pen and seven sheets of foolscap paper I started off for Pope's Court.

"Well, to my surprise and delight everything was as right as possible. The table was set out ready for me, and Mr. Duncan Ross was there to see that I got fairly to work. He started me off upon the letter A, and then he left me; but he would drop in from time to time to see that all was right with me. At two o'clock he bade me good-day, complimented me upon the amount that I had written, and locked the door of the office after me.

"This went on day after day, Mr. Holmes, and on Saturday, the manager came in and planked down four golden sovereigns for my week's work. It was the same next week, and the

Fortunate – *Lucky*
Persuade – Urge, *Influence*
Hoax – *Trick*

same the week after. Every morning, I was there at ten, and every afternoon, I left at two. By degrees, Mr. Duncan Ross took to coming in only once of a morning, and then, after a time, he did not come in at all. Still, of course, I never dared to leave the room for an instant, for I was not sure when he might come, and the billet was such a good one, and suited me so well, that I would not risk the loss of it.

"Eight weeks passed away like this, and I had written about Abbots, and Archery, and Armor, and Architecture, and Attica, and hoped with *diligence* that I might get on to the Bs before very long. It cost me something in foolscap, and I had pretty nearly filled a shelf with my writings. And then suddenly, the whole business came to an end."

"To an end?"

"Yes, sir. And no later than this morning. I went to my work as usual at ten o'clock, but the door was shut and locked, with a little square of cardboard hammered onto the middle of the panel with a tack. Here it is, and you can read for yourself."

He held up a piece of white cardboard, about the size of a sheet of note paper. It read in this fashion:

"THE RED-HEADED LEAGUE IS *DISSOLVED*.

Oct. 9, 1890."

Sherlock Holmes and I *surveyed* this *curt* announcement and the *rueful* face behind it, until the comical side of the affair so completely overtopped every consideration that we both burst out into a roar of laughter.

"I cannot see that there is anything very funny," cried our client, flushing up to the roots of his flaming head. "If you can do nothing better than laugh at me, I can go elsewhere."

"No, no," cried Holmes, shoving him back into the chair from which he had half risen. "I really wouldn't miss your case for the world. It is most refreshingly unusual. But there is, if you will excuse my saying so, something just a little funny about it. Pray what steps did you take when you found the card upon the door?"

"I was staggered, sir. I did not know what to do. Then I called at the offices round, but none of them seemed to know anything about it. Finally, I went to the landlord, who is an accountant living on the ground floor, and I asked him if he could tell me what had become of the Red-headed League.

Diligence - *Constant and earnest effort*
Dissolve – *Melt, Closed down*
Surveyed – *Reviewed*
Curt – *Abrupt*
Rueful – *Regretful*

He said that he had never heard of any such body. Then I asked him who Mr. Duncan Ross was. He answered that the name was new to him.

"'Well,' said I, 'the gentleman at No. 4.'

"'What, the red-headed man?'

"'Yes.' "'Oh,' said he, 'his name was William Morris. He was a solicitor, and was using my room as a temporary convenience until his new premises were ready. He moved out yesterday.'

"'Where could I find him?'

"'Oh, at his new offices. He did tell me the address. Yes, 17 King Edward Street, near St. Paul's.'

"I started off, Mr. Holmes, but when I got to that address it was a manufactory of *artificial* knee-caps, and no one in it had ever heard of either Mr. William Morris or Mr. Duncan Ross."

"And what did you do then?" asked Holmes.

"I went home to Saxe-Coburg Square, and I took the *advice* of my assistant. But he could not help me in any way. He could only say that if I waited I should hear by post. But that was not quite good enough, Mr. Holmes. I did not wish to lose such a place without a struggle, so, as I had heard that you were good enough to give advice to poor folk who were in need of it, I came right away to you."

"And you did very wisely," said Holmes. "Your case is an exceedingly remarkable one, and I shall be happy to look into it. From what you have told me I think that it is possible that graver issues hang from it than might at first sight appear."

"Grave enough!" said Mr. Jabez Wilson. "Why, I have lost four pounds a week."

"As far as you are personally concerned," remarked Holmes, "I do not see that you have any *grievance* against this extraordinary league. On the contrary, you are, as I understand, richer by some thirty pounds, to say nothing of the minute knowledge which you have gained on every subject which comes under the letter A. You have lost nothing by them."

"No, sir. But I want to find out about them, and who they are, and what their object was in playing this prank - if it was a *prank* - upon me. It was a pretty expensive joke for them, for it cost them two-and-thirty pounds."

Artificial – *Fake*
Advice – *Recommendation*
Grievance – *Accusation*
Prank – *Trick*

"We shall endeavour to clear up these points for you. And, first, one or two questions, Mr. Wilson. This assistant of yours who first called your attention to the advertisement - how long had he been with you?"

"About a month then."

"How did he come?"

"In answer to an advertisement."

"Was he the only applicant?"

"No, I had a dozen."

"Why did you pick him?"

"Because he was handy and would come cheap."

"At half wages, in fact."

"Yes." "What is he like, this Vincent Spaulding?"

"Small, **stout**-built, very quick in his ways, no hair on his face, though he's not short of thirty. Has a white splash of acid upon his forehead."

Holmes sat up in his chair in considerable excitement. "I thought as much," said he. "Have you ever observed that his ears are pierced for earrings?"

"Yes, sir. He told me that a gypsy had done it for him when he was a lad."

"Hum!" said Holmes, sinking back in deep thought. "He is still with you?"

"Oh, yes, sir; I have only just left him."

"And has your business been attended to in your absence?"

"Nothing to complain of, sir. There's never very much to do of a morning."

"That will do, Mr. Wilson. I shall be happy to give you an opinion upon the subject in the course of a day or two. Today is Saturday, and I hope that by Monday, we may come to a *conclusion*."

"Well, Watson," said Holmes, when our visitor had left us, "what do you make of it all?"

"I make nothing of it," I answered frankly. "It is a most mysterious business."

Conclusion – End
Bizarre – *Weird*
Commonplace –
Ordinary

"As a rule," said Holmes, "the more *bizarre* a thing is, the less mysterious it proves to be. It is your *commonplace*, feature-less crimes which are really puzzling, just as a commonplace face is the most difficult to identify. But I must be *prompt* over this matter."

"What are you going to do, then?" I asked.

"To smoke," he answered. "It is quite a three-pipe problem, and I beg that you won't speak to me for fifty minutes." He curled himself up in his chair, with his thin knees drawn up to his hawklike nose, and there he sat with his eyes closed and his black clay pipe *thrusting* out like the bill of some strange bird. I had come to the conclusion that he had dropped asleep, and indeed was nodding myself, when he suddenly sprang out of his chair with the *gesture* of a man who has made up his mind, and put his pipe down upon the mantelpiece.

"Sarasate plays at St. James's Hall this afternoon," he remarked. "What do you think, Watson? Could your patients spare you for a few hours?"

"I have nothing to do today. My practice is never very absorbing."

"Then put on your hat and come. I am going through the City first, and we can have some lunch on the way. I observe that there is a good deal of German music on the programme, which is rather more to my taste than Italian or French. It is introspective, and I want to introspect. Come along!"

We travelled by the Underground as far as Aldersgate; and a short walk took us to Saxe-Coburg Square, the scene of the singular story which we had listened to in the morning. It was a poky, little, shabby-genteel place, where four lines of dingy, two-storied brick houses looked out into a small railed-in inclosure, where a lawn of weedy grass, and a few clumps of faded laurel bushes made a hard fight against a smoke-laden and uncongenial atmosphere. Three gilt balls and a brown board with JABEZ WILSON in white letters, upon a corner house, announced the place where our red-headed client carried on his business.

Sherlock Holmes stopped in front of it with his head on one side, and looked it all over, with his eyes shining brightly between *puckered* lids. Then he walked slowly up the street, and then down again to the corner, still looking keenly at the houses. Finally he returned to the pawnbroker's and, having thumped vigorously upon the pavement with his stick two

Prompt – *Without delay*
Thrusting – *Pushing*
Gesture – *Sign*
Puckered – *Wrinkled*

or three times, he went up to the door and knocked. It was instantly opened by a bright-looking, clean-shaven young fellow, who asked him to step in.

"Thank you," said Holmes, "I only wished to ask you how you would go from here to the Strand." "Third right, fourth left," answered the assistant, promptly, closing the door.

"Smart fellow, that," observed Holmes as we walked away. "He is, in my judgement, the fourth smartest man in London, and for daring I am not sure that he has not a claim to be third. I have known something of him before."

"Evidently," said I, "Mr. Wilson's assistant counts for a good deal in this mystery of the Red-headed League. I am sure that you inquired your way merely in order that you might see him."

"Not him."

"What then?"

"The knees of his trousers."

"And what did you see?"

"What I expected to see."

"Why did you beat the pavement?"

"My dear doctor, this is a time for **observation**, not for talk. We are spies in an enemy's country. We know something of Saxe-Coburg Square. Let us now explore the parts which lie behind it."

The road in which we found ourselves as we turned around the corner from the retired Saxe-Coburg Square presented as great a **contrast** to it as the front of a picture does to the back. It was one of the main arteries which convey the traffic of the City to the north and west. The roadway was blocked with the **immense** stream of commerce flowing in a double tide inward and outward, while the footpaths were black with the hurrying swarm of pedestrians.

It was difficult to realise, as we looked at the line of fine shops and stately business premises, that they really **abutted** on the other side upon the faded and stagnant square which we had just quitted.

Abutted - *Came to an end*
Observation – *Surveillance*
Contrast – *Difference*
Immense – *huge*

"Let me see," said Holmes, standing at the corner, and glancing along the line, "I should like just to remember the order of the houses here. It is a hobby of mine to have an exact knowledge of London. There is Mortimer's, the tobacconist;

the little newspaper shop, the Coburg branch of the City and Suburban Bank, the Vegetarian Restaurant, and McFarlane's carriage-building depot. That carries us right on to the other block. And now, doctor, we've done our work, so it's time we had some play. A sandwich and a cup of coffee, and then off to violin-land, where all is sweetness, and *delicacy*, and *harmony*, and there are no red-headed clients to *vex* us with their *conundrums*."

My friend was an enthusiastic musician, being himself not only a very capable performer, but a composer of no ordinary merit. All the afternoon he sat in the stalls wrapped in the most perfect happiness, gently waving his long thin fingers in time to the music, while his gently smiling face and his languid, dreamy eyes were as unlike those of Holmes the sleuth-hound, Holmes the relentless, keen-witted, ready-handed criminal agent, as it was possible to *conceive*. In his singular character, the dual nature alternately asserted itself, and his extreme exactness and *astuteness* represented, as I have often thought, the reaction against the poetic and contemplative mood which occasionally predominated in him. The swing of his nature took him from extreme languor to devouring energy; and, as I knew well, he was never so truly formidable as when, for days on end, he had been lounging in his armchair amid his improvisations and his black-letter editions.

Then it was that the lust of the chase would suddenly come upon him, and that his brilliant reasoning power would rise to the level of intuition, until those who were unacquainted with his methods would look *askance* at him as on a man whose knowledge was not that of other mortals.

When I saw him that afternoon so enwrapped in the music at St. James's Hall, I felt that an evil time might be coming upon those whom he had set himself to hunt down.

"You want to go home, no doubt, doctor," he remarked, as we emerged.

"Yes, it would be as well."

"And I have some business to do which will take some hours. This business at Saxe-Coburg Square is serious."

"Why serious?"

"A considerable crime is in contemplation. I have every reason to believe that we shall be in time to stop it. But today

Delicacy – *Fragility*
Harmony – *Agreement*
Vex – *Displease*
Conundrum – *Puzzle*
Conceive – *To from a notion or opinion*
Astute – *Shrewd*
Askance – *Doubtfully*

being Saturday rather complicates matters. I shall want your help tonight."

"At what time?"

"Ten will be early enough."

"I shall be at Baker Street at ten."

"Very well. And, I say, doctor! there may be some little danger, so kindly put your army revolver in your pocket." He waved his hand, turned on his heel, and disappeared in an instant among the crowd.

I trust that I am not more dense than my neighbours, but I was always *oppressed* with a sense of my own stupidity in my dealings with Sherlock Holmes. Here I had heard what he had heard, I had seen what he had seen, and yet from his words that it was evident that he saw clearly not only what had happened, but what was about to happen, while to me the whole business was still confused and *grotesque*. As I drove home to my house in Kensington I thought over it all, from the extraordinary story of the red-headed copier of the "Encyclopaedia" down to the visit to Saxe-Coburg Square, and the *ominous* words with which he had parted from me. What was this *nocturnal expedition*, and why should I go armed?

Where were we going, and what were we to do? I had the hint from Holmes that this smooth-faced pawnbroker's assistant was a formidable man — a man who might play a deep game. I tried to puzzle it out, but gave it up in despair, and set the matter aside until night should bring an explanation.

It was a quarter-past nine when I started from home and made my way across the Park, and so through Oxford Street to Baker Street. Two *hansoms* were standing at the door, and, as I entered the passage, I heard the sound of voices from above.

On entering his room, I found Holmes in animated conversation with two men, one of whom I recognised as Peter Jones, the official police agent; while the other was a long, thin, sad-faced man, with a very shiny hat and oppressively respectable frock coat.

"Ha! our party is complete," said Holmes, buttoning up his pea-jacket, and taking his heavy hunting crop from the rack. "Watson, I think you know Mr. Jones, of Scotland Yard?

Hansom - *A type of carriage with two wheels, pulled by a horse*

Oppress – *Dominate*

Grotesque – *Ugly*

Ominous – *Threatening*

Nocturnal – *Night-time*

Expedition – *Journey*

Let me introduce you to Mr. Merryweather, who is to be our companion in tonight's adventure."

"We're hunting in couples again, doctor, you see," said Jones, in his consequential way. "Our friend here is a wonderful man for starting a chase. All he wants is an old dog to help him do the running down."

"I hope a wild goose may not prove to be the end of our chase," observed Mr. Merryweather *gloomily*. "You may place considerable confidence in Mr. Holmes, sir," said the police agent *loftily*. "He has his own little methods, which are, if he won't mind my saying so, just a little too theoretical and fantastic, but he has the makings of a detective in him. It is not too much to say that once or twice, as in that business of the Sholto murder and the Agra treasure, he has been more nearly correct than the official force."

"Oh, if you say so, Mr. Jones, it is all right!" said the stranger, with *deference*. "Still, I confess that I miss my rubber. It is the first Saturday night for seven-and-twenty years that I have not had my rubber."

"I think you will find," said Sherlock Holmes, "that you will play for a higher stake tonight than you have ever done yet, and that the play will be more exciting. For you, Mr. Merryweather, the stake will be some thirty thousand pounds; and for you, Jones, it will be the man upon whom you wish to lay your hands."

"John Clay, the murderer, thief, smasher, and forger. He's a young man, Mr. Merryweather, but he is at the head of his profession, and I would rather have my bracelets on him than on any criminal in London.

He's a remarkable man, is young John Clay. His grandfather was a Royal Duke, and he himself has been to Eton and Oxford. His brain is as *cunning* as his fingers, and though we meet signs of him at every turn, we never know where to find the man himself. He'll crack a crib in Scotland one week, and be raising money to build an orphanage in Cornwall the next. I've been on his track for years, and have never set eyes on him yet."

"I hope that I may have the pleasure of introducing you tonight. I've had one or two little turns also with Mr. John Clay, and I agree with you that he is at the head of his profession. It is past ten, however, and quite time that we started. If

Deference - *Respect*
Gloomy – *Dark*
Loftily – *Superciliously*
Cunning – *Slyness*

you two will take the first hansom, Watson and I will follow in the second."

Sherlock Holmes was not very communicative during the long drive, and lay back in the cab humming the tunes which he had heard in the afternoon. We rattled through an endless *labyrinth* of gaslit streets until we emerged into Farringdon Street.

"We are close there now," my friend remarked. "This fellow Merryweather is a bank director and personally interested in the matter. I thought it as well to have Jones with us also. He is not a bad fellow, though an absolute *imbecile* in his profession. He has one positive virtue. He is as brave as a bulldog, and as *tenacious* as a lobster if he gets his claws upon anyone. Here we are, and they are waiting for us."

We had reached the same crowded thoroughfare in which we had found ourselves in the morning. Our cabs were dismissed, and following the guidance of Mr. Merryweather, we passed down a narrow passage, and through a side door which he opened for us. Within there was a small corridor, which ended in a very *massive* iron gate.

This also was opened, and led down a flight of winding stone steps, which terminated at another formidable gate. Mr. Merryweather stopped to light a lantern, and then conducted us down a dark, earth-smelling passage, and so, after opening a third door, into a huge vault or cellar, which was piled all around with crates and massive boxes.

"You are not very vulnerable from above," Holmes remarked, as he held up the lantern and gazed about him.

"Nor from below," said Mr. Merryweather, striking his stick upon the flags which lined the floor. "Why, dear me, it sounds quite hollow!" he remarked, looking up in surprise.

"I must really ask you to be a little more quiet," said Holmes severely. "You have already *imperiled* the whole success of our expedition. Might I beg that you would have the goodness to sit down upon one of those boxes, and not to *interfere*?"

The solemn Mr. Merryweather *perched* himself upon a crate, with a very injured expression upon his face, while Holmes fell upon his knees upon the floor, and, with the lantern and a magnifying lens, began to examine minutely the cracks between the stones. A few seconds sufficed to satisfy

Labyrinth – *Maze*
Tenacious –
Stubborn
Massive – *Huge*
Imperil – *Endanger*
Interfere – *Hinder*
Perch – *Alight*
Imbecile - *Weak -
minded*

him, for he sprang to his feet again, and put his glass in his pocket.

"We have at least an hour before us," he remarked, "for they can hardly take any steps until the good pawnbroker is safely in bed. Then they will not lose a minute, for the sooner they do their work the longer time they will have for their escape.

We are at present, doctor - as no doubt you have divined - in the cellar of the City branch of one of the principal London banks. Mr. Merryweather is the chairman of directors, and he will explain to you that there are reasons why the more daring criminals of London should take a considerable interest in this cellar at present."

"It is our French gold," whispered the director. "We have had several warnings that an attempt might be made upon it."

"Your French gold?"

"Yes. We had occasion some months ago to strengthen our resources, and *borrowed*, for that purpose, thirty thousand napoleons from the Bank of France. It has become known that we have never had occasion to unpack the money, and that it is still lying in our cellar.

The crate upon which I sit contains two thousand napoleons packed between layers of lead foil. Our reserve of bullion is much larger at present than is usually kept in a single branch office, and the directors have had misgivings upon the subject."

"Which were very well *justified*," observed Holmes. "And now it is time that we arranged our little plans. I expect that within an hour, matters will come to a head. In the meantime, Mr. Merryweather, we must put the screen over that dark lantern."

"And sit in the dark?"

"I am afraid so. I had brought a pack of cards in my pocket, and I thought that, as we were a partie carree, you might have your rubber after all. But I see that the enemy's preparations have gone so far that we cannot risk the presence of a light. And, first of all, we must choose our positions.

These are daring men, and, though we shall take them at a disadvantage, they may do us some harm, unless we are careful. I shall stand behind this crate, and do you conceal

Borrow – *Have a loan of*
Justified – *Necessary*
Crouch – *Bend*
Assure – *Promise*

yourself behind those. Then, when I flash a light upon them, close in swiftly. If they fire, Watson, have no compunction about shooting them down."

I placed my revolver, cocked, upon the top of the wooden case behind which I *crouched*. Holmes shot the slide across the front of his lantern, and left us in pitch darkness - such an absolute darkness as I have never before experienced. The smell of hot metal remained to *assure* us that the light was still there, ready to flash out at a moment's notice. To me, with my nerves worked up to a pitch of expectancy, there was something depressing and subduing in the sudden gloom, and in the cold, dank air of the vault.

"They have but one *retreat*," whispered Holmes. "That is back through the house into Saxe-Coburg Square. I hope that you have done what I asked you, Jones?"

"I have an inspector and two officers waiting at the front door."

"Then we have stopped all the holes. And now we must be silent and wait."

What a time it seemed! From comparing notes afterwards, it was but an hour and a quarter, yet it appeared to me that the night must have almost gone, and the dawn be breaking above us.

My limbs were weary and stiff, for I feared to change my position, yet my nerves were worked up to the highest pitch of tension, and my hearing was so *acute* that I could not only hear the gentle breathing of my companions, but I could distinguish the deeper, heavier inbreath of the bulky Jones from the thin, sighing note of the bank director. From my position, I could look over the case in the direction of the floor. Suddenly my eyes caught the glint of a light.

At first it was but a *lurid* spark upon the stone pavement. Then it lengthened out until it became a yellow line, and then, without any warning or sound, a gash seemed to open and a hand appeared, a white, almost womanly hand, which felt about in the center of the little area of light. For a minute or more the hand, with its writhing fingers, *protruded* out of the floor.

Then it was withdrawn as suddenly as it appeared, and all was dark again save the single lurid spark, which marked a chink between the stones.

Retreat – *Move away*
Acute – *Sharp*
Lurid – *Gruesome,*
Horrible
Protrude – *Stick out,*
To project
Momentary – *Brief*
Lithe – *Supple*

Holmes bla

d, with the

ough I see

atson," he e

sat over a g

erfectly obv

f this rather

gue, and th

is not over-

The man's business was a small one, and there was nothing in his house which could account for such elaborate preparations, and such an expenditure as they were at. It must then be something out of the house. What could it be? I thought of the assistant's fondness for photography, and his trick of vanishing into the cellar. The cellar! There was the end of this tangled cleu.

Then I made inquiries as to this mysterious assistant, and found that I had to deal with one of the coolest and most daring criminals in London. He was doing something in the cellar - something which took many hours a day for months on end. What could it be, once more? I could think of nothing save that he was running a tunnel to some other building.

"So far I had got when we went to visit the scene of action. I surprised you by beating upon the pavement with my stick. I was *ascertaining* whether the cellar stretched out in front or behind. It was not in front.

Then I rang the bell, and, as I hoped, the assistant answered it. We have had some skirmishes, but we had never set eyes upon each other before. I hardly looked at his face. His knees were what I wished to see. You must yourself have remarked how worn, wrinkled, and stained they were. They spoke of those hours of burrowing.

The only remaining point was what they were *burrowing* for. I walked around the corner, saw that the City and the Suburban Bank abutted on our friend's premises, and felt that I had solved my problem. When you drove home after the concert I called upon Scotland Yard, and upon the chairman of the bank directors, with the result that you have seen."

"And how could you tell that they would make their attempt tonight?" I asked. "Well, when they closed their League offices that was a sign that they cared no longer about Mr. Jabez Wilson's presence; in other words, that they had completed their tunnel. But it was essential that they should use it soon, as it might be discovered, or the bullion might be removed. Saturday would suit them better than any other day, as it would give them two days for their escape. For all these reasons, I expected them to come tonight."

"You reasoned it out beautifully," I exclaimed, in *unfeigned admiration*. "It is so long a chain, and yet every link rings true."

Ascertain – *Determine*
Burrow – *Hole, A place of retreat*
Feign – *Pretend*
Admiration – *High regard*

"It saved me from *ennui*," he answered, yawning. "Alas! I already feel it closing in upon me. My life is spent in one long effort to escape from the commonplaces of existence. These little problems help me to do so."

"And you are a benefactor of the race," said I. He shrugged his shoulders. "Well, perhaps, after all, it is of some little use," he remarked. "'L'homme c'est rien - l'oeuvre c'est tout,' as Gustave Flaubert wrote to Georges Sands."

Food For Thought

Would Holmes be able to successfully solve this strange case without the assistance of the police and Mr. Merryweather, chairman of directors of one of the principal Landon banks?

Ennui – *Boredom*
Yawning – *To open the mouth wide and take in air deeply due to tiredness*
Benefactor – *Patron, Supporter*

An Understanding

Q. 1. "I don't know that your assistant is not as remarkable as your advertisement." Who spoke these words to whom and why?
Ans. _____
_____
_____
_____
_____

Q. 2. "This business at Saxe-Coburg Square is serious. "Why did Sherlock Holmes say so to the author, Dr. Arthur Conan Doyle?
Ans. _____
_____
_____
_____
_____

Q. 3. How did Holmes guess the actual motive of John Clay when he heard of the assistant working for half wages in Jabez Wilson's small pawn broker's business at Saxe-Coburg Square, near the city?
Ans. _____
_____
_____
_____
_____

Q. 4. How did the assistant's fondness for photography, and his trick of vanishing into the cellar act as important clues in solving this mystery of the Red- Headed League?
Ans. _____
_____
_____
_____
_____

nsieur Dub

the well-kn

d their ener

century wil

ely told. Me

n promised

Foreign Office, and then he passed completely out of my mind until the following letter recalled his existence:

Briarbrae, Woking

My dear Watson,

I have no doubt that you can remember, "Tadpole" Phelps, who was in the fifth form when you were in the third. It is possible even that you may have heard that through my uncle's influence, I obtained a good appointment at the Foreign Office, and that I was in a situation of trust and honour until a horrible misfortune came suddenly to blast my career.

There is no use writing of the details of that dreadful event. In the event of your *acceding* to my request it is probably that I shall have to narrate them to you. I have only just recovered from nine weeks of brain-fever, and am still exceedingly weak. Do you think that you could bring your friend, Mr. Holmes down to see me? I should like to have his opinion of the case, though the authorities assure me that nothing more can be done. Do try to bring him down, and as soon as possible. Every minute seems an hour, while I live in this state of horrible suspense. Assure him that if I have not asked his advice sooner, it was not because I did not appreciate his talents, but because I have been off my head ever since the blow fell. Now I am clear again, though I dare not think of it too much for fear of a relapse. I am still so weak that I have to write, as you see, by dictating. Do try to bring him.

Your old school fellow,

Percy Phelps.

There was something that touched me as I read this letter, something pitiable in the reiterated appeals to bring Holmes. So moved was I that even had it been a difficult matter, I should have tried it, but of course, I knew well that Holmes loved his art, so that he was ever as ready to bring his aid as his client could be to receive it. My wife agreed with me that not a moment should be lost in laying the matter before him, and so within an hour of breakfast time, I found myself back once more in the old rooms in Baker Street.

Holmes was seated at his side table clad in his dressing-gown, and working hard over a chemical *investigation*. A large curved retort was boiling furiously in the bluish flame

Accede – *Agree*
Investigation – *Inquiry*

of a Bunsen burner, and the distilled drops were condensing into a two-litre measure. My friend hardly *glanced* up as I entered, and I, seeing that his investigation must be of importance, seated myself in an armchair and waited. He dipped into this bottle or that, drawing out a few drops of each with his glass pipette, and finally brought a test tube containing a solution over to the table. In his right hand, he held a slip of litmus paper.

"You come at a *crisis*, Watson," said he. "If this paper remains blue, all is well. If it turns red, it means a man's life." He dipped it into the test tube and it flushed at once into a dull, dirty crimson. "Hum! I thought as much!" he cried. "I will be at your service in an instant, Watson. You will find tobacco in the Persian slipper." He turned to his desk and scribbled off several telegrams, which were handed over to the pageboy. Then he threw himself down into the chair opposite, and drew up his knees until his fingers clasped, round his long, thin shins.

"A very commonplace little murder," said he. "You've got something better, I fancy. You are the stormy petrel of crime, Watson. What is it?"

I handed him the letter, which he read with the most concentrated attention.

"It does not tell us very much, does it?" he remarked, as he handed it back to me.

"Hardly anything."

"And yet the writing is of interest."

"But the writing is not his own."

"Precisely. It is a woman's."

"A man's surely," I cried.

"No, a woman's, and a woman of rare character. You see, at the *commencement* of an investigation, it is something to know that your client is in close contact with someone who, for good or evil, has an exceptional nature. My interest is already awakened in the case. If you are ready, we will start at once for Woking, and see this diplomatist who is in such evil case, and the lady to whom he dictates his letters."

We were fortunate enough to catch an early train at Waterloo, and in a little under an hour, we found ourselves among the fir-woods and the heather of Woking. Briarbrae

Glance – *A quick look*
Crisis – *Disaster*
Commence – *Begin*

proved to be a large detached house standing in extensive grounds within a few minutes' walk of the station. On sending in our cards, we were shown into an elegantly appointed drawing room, where we were joined in a few minutes by a rather stout man who received us with much **hospitality**. His age may have been nearer forty than thirty, but his cheeks were so ruddy and his eyes so merry that he still conveyed the impression of a plump and mischievous boy.

"I am so glad that you have come," said he, shaking our hands with **effusion**. "Percy has been inquiring for you all morning. Ah, poor old chap, he clings to any straw! His father and his mother asked me to see you, for the mere mention of the subject is very painful to them."

"We have had no details yet," observed Holmes. "I perceive that you are not yourself a member of the family."

Our acquaintance looked surprised, and then, glancing down, he began to laugh.

"Of course you saw the J H monogram on my locket," said he. "For a moment, I thought you had done something clever. Joseph Harrison is my name, and as Percy is to marry my sister, Annie I shall at least be a relation by marriage. You will find my sister in his room, for she has nursed him hand-and-foot this two months back. Perhaps, we'd better go in at once, for I know how impatient he is."

The chamber in which we were shown was on the same floor as the drawing room. It was furnished partly as a sitting and partly as a bedroom, with flowers arranged **daintily** in every nook and corner. A young man, very pale and worn, was lying upon a sofa near the open window, through which came the rich scent of the garden and the balmy summer air. A woman was sitting beside him, who rose as we entered.

"Shall I leave, Percy?" she asked.

He clutched her hand to detain her. "How are you, Watson?" said he, cordially. "I should never have known you under that moustache, and I dare say you would not be prepared to swear to me. This I **presume** is your celebrated friend, Mr. Sherlock Holmes?"

I introduced him in a few words, and we both sat down. The stout young man had left us, but his sister still remained with her hand in that of the invalid. She was a striking-looking woman, a little short and thick for symmetry, but with a beautiful

Effusion - *Pouring forth*
Hospitality - *A friendly reception*
Dainty – *Delicate*
Presume – *Assume*

olive complexion, large, dark, Italian eyes, and a wealth of deep black hair. Her rich tints made the white face of her companion the more worn and haggard by the contrast.

"I won't waste your time," said he, raising himself upon the sofa. "I'll *plunge* into the matter without further preamble. I was a happy and successful man, Mr. Holmes, and on the eve of being married, when a sudden and dreadful *misfortune* wrecked all my prospects in life.

"I was, as Watson may have told you, in the Foreign Office, and through the influences of my uncle, Lord Holdhurst, I rose rapidly to a responsible position. When my uncle became foreign minister in this administration he gave me several missions of trust, and as I always brought them to a successful conclusion, he came at last to have the utmost confidence in my ability and tact.

"Nearly ten weeks ago -- to be more accurate, on the 23rd of May -- he called me into his private room, and, after complimenting me on the good work which I had done, he informed me that he had a new commission of trust for me to execute.

"'This,' said he, taking a gray roll of paper from his bureau, 'is the original of that secret treaty between England and Italy of which, I regret to say, some rumours have already got into the public press. It is of enormous importance that nothing further should leak out. The French or the Russian embassy would pay an immense sum to learn the contents of these papers. They should not leave my bureau were it not that it is absolutely necessary to have them copied. You have a desk in your office?'

"'Yes, sir.'

"'Then take the treaty and lock it up there. I shall give directions that you may remain behind when the others go, so that you may copy it at your *leisure* without the fear of being overlooked. When you have finished, relock both the original and the draft in the desk, and hand them over to me personally tomorrow morning.'

"I took the papers and --"

"Excuse me an instant," said Holmes. "Were you alone during this conversation?"

"Absolutely." "In a large room?"

"Thirty feet each way."

Plunge - *Jump*
Misfortune – *Bad luck*
Leisure – *Free time*

"In the centre?"

"Yes, about it."

"And speaking low?"

"My uncle's voice is always remarkably low. I hardly spoke at all."

"Thank you," said Holmes, shutting his eyes; "pray go on."

"I did exactly what he indicated, and waited until the other clerks had departed. One of them in my room, Charles Gorot, had some arrears of work to make up, so I left him there and went out to dine. When I returned, he was gone. I was *anxious* to hurry my work, for I knew that Joseph -- the Mr. Harrison whom you saw just now -- was in town, and that he would travel down to Woking by the eleven o'clock train, and I wanted if possible to catch it.

"When I came to examine the treaty I saw at once that it was of such importance that my uncle had been guilty of no *exaggeration* in what he had said. Without going into details, I may say that it defined the position of Great Britain towards the Triple Alliance, and foreshadowed the policy which this country would pursue in the event of the French fleet gaining a complete ascendancy over that of Italy in the Mediterranean. The questions treated in it were purely naval. At the end were the signatures of the high dignitaries who had signed it. I glanced my eyes over it, and then settled down to my task of copying.

"It was a long document, written in the French language, and containing twenty-six separate articles. I copied as quickly as I could, but at nine o'clock, I had only done nine articles, and it seemed hopeless for me to attempt to catch my train. I was feeling drowsy and stupid, partly from my dinner and also from the effects of a long day's work. A cup of coffee would clear my brain. A commissionnaire remains all night in a little lodge at the foot of the stairs, and is in the habit of making coffee at his spirit-lamp for any of the officials who may be working over time. I rang the bell, therefore, to summon him.

"To my surprise, it was a woman who answered the summons, a large, coarse-faced, elderly woman, in an apron. She explained that she was the commissionnaire's wife, who did the charing, and I gave her the order for the coffee.

Anxious – *Nervous*
Exaggeration –
Overstatement

"I wrote two more articles and then, feeling more drowsy than ever, I rose and walked up and down the room to stretch my legs. My coffee had not yet come, and I wondered what was the cause of the delay could be. Opening the door, I started down the corridor to find out. There was a straight passage, dimly lighted, which led from the room in which I had been working, and was the only exit from it. It ended in a curving staircase, with the commissionnaire's lodge in the passage at the bottom. Halfway down this staircase is a small landing, with another passage running into it at right angles. This second one leads by means of a second small stair to a side door, used by servants, and also as a short — cut by clerks when coming from Charles Street. Here is a rough chart of the place."

"Thank you. I think that I quite follow you," said Sherlock Holmes.

"It is of the utmost importance that you should notice this point. I went down the stairs and into the hall, where I found the commissionnaire fast asleep in his box, with the kettle boiling furiously upon the spirit-lamp. I took off the kettle and blew out the lamp, for the water was spurting over the floor. Then I put out my hand and was about to shake the man, who was still sleeping soundly, when a bell over his head rang loudly, and he woke with a start.

"'Mr. Phelps, sir!' said he, looking at me in *bewilderment*.

"'I came down to see if my coffee was ready.'

"'I was boiling the kettle when I fell asleep, sir.' He looked at me and then up at the still *quivering* bell with an ever-grow-ing *astonishment* upon his face.

"'If you was here, sir, then who rang the bell?' he asked.

"'The bell!' I cried. 'What bell is it?'

"'It's the bell of the room you were working in.'

"A cold hand seemed to close around my heart. Someone, then, was in that room where my precious treaty lay upon the table. I ran *frantically* up the stair and along the passage. There was no one in the corridors, Mr. Holmes. There was no one in the room. All was exactly as I left it, save only that the papers which had been committed to my care had been taken from the desk on which they lay. The copy was there, and the original was gone."

Bewilderment – *Confusion*
Quiver – *Tremble*
Astonishment – *Surprise*
Frantic – *Desperate, Frenzied*

Holmes sat up in his chair and rubbed his hands. I could see that the problem was entirely to his heart. "Pray, what did you do then?" he *murmured*.

"I recognised in an instant that the thief must have come up the stairs from the side door. Of course, I must have met, him if he had come the other way."

"You were satisfied that he could not have been *concealed* in the room all the time, or in the corridor which you have just described as dimly lighted?"

"It is absolutely impossible. A rat could not conceal himself either in the room or the corridor. There is no cover at all."

"Thank you. Pray proceed."

"The commissionnaire, seeing by my pale face that something was to be feared, had followed me upstairs. Now we both rushed along the corridor and down the steep steps which led to Charles Street. The door at the bottom was closed, but unlocked. We flung it open and rushed out. I can distinctly remember that as we did so there came three chimes from a neighbouring clock. It was quarter to ten."

"That is of enormous importance," said Holmes, making a note upon his shirt-cuff.

"The night was very dark, and a thin, warm rain was falling. There was no one in Charles Street, but a great traffic was going on, as usual, in Whitehall, at the extremity. We rushed along the pavement, bareheaded as we were, and at the far corner, we found a policeman standing.

"'A robbery has been committed,' I gasped. 'A document of immense value has been stolen from the Foreign Office. Has anyone passed this way?'

"'I have been standing here for a quarter of an hour, sir,' said he; 'only one person has passed during that time -- a woman, tall and elderly, with a Paisley shawl.'

"'Ah, that is only my wife,' cried the commissionnaire; 'has no one else passed?'

"'No one.'

"'Then it must be the other way that the thief took,' cried the fellow, tugging at my sleeve.

"'But I was not satisfied, and the attempts which he made to draw me away increased my suspicions. "'Which way did the woman go?' I cried.

Murmur – *Speak softly*
Conceal – *Hide*

"'I don't know, sir. I noticed her pass, but I had no special reason for watching her. She seemed to be in a hurry.'

"'How long ago was it?'

"'Oh, not very many minutes.'

"'Within the last five?'

"'Well, it could not be more than five.'

"'You're only wasting your time, sir, and every minute now is of importance,' cried the commissionnaire; 'take my word for it that my old woman has nothing to do with it, and come down to the other end of the street. Well, if you won't, I will.' And with that he rushed off in the other direction.

"But I was after him in an instant and caught him by the sleeve.

"'Where do you live?' said I.

"'16 Ivy Lane, Brixton,' he answered. 'But don't let yourself be drawn away upon a *false* scent, Mr. Phelps. Come to the other end of the street and let us see if we can hear of anything.'

"Nothing was to be lost by following his *advice*. With the policeman we both hurried down, but only to find the street full of traffic, many people coming and going, but all only too eager to get to a place of safety upon so wet a night. There was no lounger who could tell us who had passed.

"Then we returned to the office, and searched the stairs and the passage without result. The corridor which led to the room was laid down with a kind of creamy linoleum which shows an impression very easily. We examined it very carefully, but found no outline of any footmark."

"Had it been raining all evening?"

"Since about seven."

"How is it, then, that the woman who came into the room about nine left no traces with her muddy boots?"

"I am glad you raised the point. It occurred to me at the time. The charwomen are in the habit of taking off their boots at the commissionnaire's office, and putting on list slippers."

"That is very clear. There were no marks, then, though the night was a wet one? The chain of events is certainly one of *extraordinary* interest. What did you do next?

"We examined the room also. There is no possibility of a secret door, and the windows are quite thirty feet from the

False – *Fake*
Advice – *Recommendation*
Extraordinary – *Unusual, Exceptional*

ground. Both of them were fastened on the inside. The carpet prevents any possibility of a trap-door, and the ceiling is of the ordinary whitewashed kind. I will **pledge** my life that whoever stole my papers could only have come through the door."

"How about the fireplace?"

"They use none. There is a stove. The bell-rope hangs from the wire just to the right of my desk. Whoever rang it must have come right up to the desk to do it. But why should any criminal wish to ring the bell? It is a most insoluble mystery."

""Certainly, the incident was unusual. What were your next steps? You examined the room, I presume, to see if the **intruder** had left any traces -- any cigar-end or dropped glove or hairpin or other trifle?"

"There was nothing of the sort."

"No smell?"

"Well, we never thought of that."

"Ah, a scent of tobacco would have been worth a great deal to us in such an investigation."

"I never smoke myself, so I think I should have observed it if there had been any smell of tobacco. There was absolutely no clue of any kind. The only **tangible** fact was that the commissionnaire's wife -- Mrs. Tangey was the name -- had hurried out of the place. He could give no explanation save that it was about the time when the woman always went home. The policeman and I agreed that our best plan would be to **seize** the woman before she could get rid of the papers, presuming that she had them.

"The alarm had reached Scotland Yard by this time, and Mr. Forbes, the detective, came around at once and took up the case with a great deal of energy. We hire a hansom, and in half an hour, we were at the address which had been given to us. A young woman opened the door, who proved to be Mrs. Tangey's eldest daughter. Her mother had not come back yet, and we were shown into the front room to wait.

"About ten minutes later, a knock came at the door, and here we made the one serious mistake for which I blame myself. Instead of opening the door ourselves, we allowed the girl to do so. We heard her say, 'Mother, there are two men in the house waiting to see you,' and an instant afterwards we heard the patter of feet rushing down the passage. Forbes flung open the door, and we both ran into the back room or

Tangible - *Real or actual*
Pledge – *Vow*
Intruder – *Imposter*
Seize – *Grab*

kitchen, but the woman had got there before us. She stared at us with **defiant** eyes, and then, suddenly recognising me, an expression of absolute astonishment came over her face.

"'Why, if it isn't Mr. Phelps, of the office!' she cried.

"'Come, come, who did you think we were when you ran away from us?' asked my companion.

"'I thought you were the brokers,' said she, 'we have had some trouble with a tradesman.'

"'That's not quite good enough,' answered Forbes. 'We have reason to believe that you have taken a paper of importance to the Foreign Office, and that you ran in here to **dispose** of it. You must come back with us to Scotland Yard to be searched.'

"It was in vain that she protested and resisted. A four-wheeler was brought, and we all three drove back in it. We had first made an examination of the kitchen, and especially of the kitchen fire, to see whether she might have made away with the papers during the instant that she was alone. There were no signs, however, of any ashes or scraps. When we reached Scotland Yard, she was handed over at once to the female searcher. I waited in an agony of suspense until she came back with her report. There were no signs of the papers.

"Then for the first time the horror of my situation came in its full force. Hitherto I had been acting, and action had numbed thought. I had been so confident of regaining the treaty at once that I had not dared to think of what would be the consequence if I failed to do so. But now there was nothing more to be done, and I had leisure to realise my position. It was horrible. Watson there would tell you that I was a nervous, sensitive boy at school. It is my nature. I thought of my uncle and of his colleagues in the Cabinet, of the shame which I had brought upon him, upon myself, upon everyone connected with me. What though I was the victim of an extraordinary accident? No allowance is made for accidents where diplomatic interests are at stake. I was ruined, shamefully, hopelessly ruined. I don't know what I did. I fancy I must have made a scene. I have a dim recollection of a group of officials who crowded around me, endeavouring to soothe me. One of them drove down with me to Waterloo, and saw me into the Woking train. I believe that he would have come all the way had it not been that Dr. Ferrier, who lives near me,

Defiant – *Disobedient*

Dispose – *Arrange*

Protest – *Complain*

Horror – *Dismay, Shock*

was going down by that very train. The doctor most kindly took charge of me, and it was well he did so, for I had a fit in the station, and before we reached home, I was practically a raving maniac.

"You can imagine the state of things here when they were roused from their beds by the doctor's ringing and found me in this condition. Poor Annie here and my mother were broken-hearted. Dr. Ferrier had just heard enough from the detective at the station to be able to give an idea of what had happened, and his story did not mend matters. It was evident to all that I was in for a long illness, so Joseph was bundled out of this cheery bedroom, and it was turned into a sick-room for me. Here I have lain, Mr. Holmes, for over nine weeks, unconscious, and raving with brain-fever. If it had not been for Miss Harrison here and for the doctor's care, I should not be speaking to you now. She has nursed me by day and a hired nurse has looked after me by night, for in my mad fits, I was capable of anything. Slowly my reason has cleared, but it is only during the last three days that my memory has quite returned. Sometimes, I wish that it never had. The first thing that I did was to wire to Mr. Forbes, who had the case in hand. He came out, and assures me that, though everything has been done, no trace of a clue has been discovered. The commissionnaire and his wife have been examined in every way without any light being thrown upon the matter. The suspicions of the police then rested upon young Gorot, who, as you may remember, stayed overtime in the office that night. His remaining behind and his French name were really the only two points which could suggest suspicion; but, as a matter of fact, I did not begin work until he had gone, and his people are of Huguenot extraction, but as English in sympathy and tradition as you and I are. Nothing was found to implicate him in any way, and there the matter dropped. I turn to you, Mr. Holmes, as absolutely my last hope. If you fail me, then my honour as well as my position are forever forfeited."

The invalid sank back upon his cushions, tired out by this long recital, while his nurse poured him out a glass of some stimulating medicine. Holmes sat silently, with his head thrown back and his eyes closed, in an attitude which might seem listless to a stranger, but which I knew betokened the most intense self-absorption.

Maniac – *Fanatic*
Mend – *Repair*
Assure – *Guarantee*
Implicate –
Associate
Betoken – *Promise*

"Your statement has been so explicit," said he at last, "that you have really left me very few questions to ask. There is one of the very utmost importance, however. Did you tell anyone that you had this special task to perform?"

"No one."

"Not Miss Harrison here, for example?"

"No. I had not been back to Woking between getting the order and executing the commission."

"And none of your people had by chance been to see you?"

"None." "Did any of them know their way about in the office?"

"Oh, yes, all of them had been shown over it."

"Still, of course, if you said nothing to anyone about the treaty, these inquiries are *irrelevant*."

"I said nothing."

"Do you know anything of the commissionnaire?"

"Nothing except that he is an old soldier."

"What regiment?"

"Oh, I have heard -- Coldstream Guards."

"Thank you. I have no doubt that I can get details from Forbes. The authorities are excellent at *amassing* facts, though they do not always use them to advantage. What a lovely thing a rose is!"

He walked past the couch to the open window, and held up the drooping stalk of a moss-rose, looking down at the dainty blend of crimson and green. It was a new phase of his character to me, for I had never before seen him show any keen interest in natural objects.

"There is nothing in which deduction is so necessary as in religion," said he, leaning with his back against the shutters. "It can be built up as an exact science by the reasoner. Our highest assurance of the goodness of Providence seems to me to rest in the flowers. All other things, our powers, our desires, our food, are all really necessary for our existence in the first instance. But this rose is an extra. Its smell and its colour are an *embellishment* of life, not a condition of it. It is only goodness which gives extras, and so I say again that we have much to hope from the flowers.

Percy Phelps and his nurse looked at Holmes during this demonstration with surprise and a good deal of *disappointment*

Irrelevant – *Beside the point*

Amass – *Collect*

Embellishment – *Decoration*

Disappoint – *Let down*

written upon their faces. He had fallen into a reverie, with the moss-rose between his fingers. It had lasted some minutes before the young lady broke in upon it.

"Do you see any prospect of solving this mystery, Mr. Holmes?" she asked, with a touch of *asperity* in her voice.

"Oh, the mystery!" he answered, coming back with a start to the realities of life. "Well, it would be **absurd** to **deny** that the case is a very **abstruse** and complicated one, but I can promise you that I will look into the matter and let you know any points which may strike me."

"Do you see any clue?"

"You have furnished me with seven, but, of course, I must test them before I can pronounce upon their value."

"You suspect someone?"

"I suspect myself."

"What!" "Of coming to conclusions too rapidly."

"Then go to London and test your conclusions."

"Your advice is very excellent, Miss Harrison," said Holmes, rising. "I think, Watson, we cannot do better. Do not allow yourself to *indulge* in false hopes, Mr. Phelps. The affair is a very tangled one."

"I shall be in a fever until I see you again," cried the diplomatist.

"Well, I'll come out by the same train tomorrow, though it's more than likely that my report will be a negative one."

"God bless you for promising to come," cried our client. "It gives me fresh life to know that something is being done. By the way, I have had a letter from Lord Holdhurst."

"Ha! What did he say?"

"He was cold, but not **harsh**. I dare say my severe illness prevented him from being that. He repeated that the matter was of the utmost importance, and added that no steps would be taken about my future -- by which he means, of course, my dismissal -- until my health was restored and I had an opportunity of repairing my misfortune."

"Well, that was reasonable and considerate," said Holmes. "Come, Watson, for we have a good day's work before us in town."

Mr. Joseph Harrison drove us down to the station, and we were soon whirling up in a Portsmouth train. Holmes was

Abstruse - *Hard to understand*
Asperity – *Harshness*
Absurd – *Ridiculous*
Deny – *Disagree with*
Indulge – *Pamper*
Harsh – *Cruel*

sunk in profound thought, and hardly opened his mouth until we had passed Clapham Junction.

"It's a very cheery thing to come into London by any of these lines which run high, and allow you to look down upon the houses like this."

I thought he was joking, for the view was sordid enough, but he soon explained himself.

"Look at those big, isolated clumps of building rising up above the slates, like brick islands in a lead-coloured sea."

"The board schools."

"Light-houses, my boy! Beacons of the future! Capsules with hundreds of bright little seeds in each, out of which will spring the wise, better England of the future. I suppose that man Phelps does not drink?"

"I should not think so."

"Nor should I, but we are bound to take every possibility into account. The poor devil has certainly got himself into very deep water, and it's a question whether we shall ever be able to get him ashore. What did you think of Miss Harrison?"

"A girl of strong character."

"Yes, but she is a good sort, or I am mistaken. She and her brother are the only children of an iron-master somewhere up Northumberland way. He got engaged to her when travelling last winter, and she came down to be introduced to his people, with her brother as escort. Then came the smash, and she stayed on to nurse her lover, while brother Joseph, finding himself pretty snug, stayed on too. I've been making a few independent inquiries, you see. But today must be a day of inquiries."

"My practice --" I began.

"Oh, if you find your own cases more interesting than mine --" said Holmes, with some asperity.

"I was going to say that my practice could get along very well for a day or two, since it is the slackest time in the year."

"Excellent," said he, recovering his good humour. "Then we'll look into this matter together. I think that we should begin by seeing Forbes. He can probably tell us all the details we want until we know from what side the case is to be approached.

"You said you had a clue?"

Profound –
Thoughtful
Sordid – Disgusting
Escort – Accompany

"Well, we have several, but we can only test their value by further inquiry. The most difficult crime to track is the one which is purposeless. Now this is not purposeless. Who is it who profits by it? There is the French ambassador, there is the Russian, there is whoever might sell it to either of these, and there is Lord Holdhurst."

"Lord Holdhurst!"

"Well, it is just **conceivable** that a statesman might find himself in a position where he was not sorry to have such a document accidentally destroyed."

"Not a statesman with the honourable record of Lord Holdhurst?"

"It is a possibility and we cannot afford to **disregard** it. We shall see the noble lord today and find out if he can tell us anything. Meanwhile, I have already set inquiries on foot."

"Already?" "Yes, I sent wires from Woking station to every evening paper in London. This advertisement will appear in each of them."

He handed over a sheet torn from a notebook. On it was scribbled in pencil: "L10 reward. The number of the cab which dropped a fare at or about the door of the Foreign Office in Charles Street at quarter to ten in the evening of May 23rd. Apply 221 B, Baker Street."

"You are confident that the thief came in a cab?"

"If not, there is no harm done. But if Mr. Phelps is correct in stating that there is no hiding place either in the room or the corridors, then the person must have come from outside. If he came from outside on so wet a night, and yet left no trace of damp upon the linoleum, which was examined within a few minutes of his passing, then it is exceeding probably that he came in a cab. Yes, I think that we may safely deduce a cab."

"It sounds **plausible**."

"That is one of the clues of which I spoke. It may lead us to something. And then, of course, there is the bell -- which is the most distinctive feature of the case. Why should the bell ring? Was it the thief who did it out of bravado? Or was it someone who was with the thief who did it in order to prevent the crime? Or was it an accident? Or was it -- ?" He sank back into the state of **intense** and silent thought from which

Conceivable –
Imaginable
Disregard – *Ignore*
Plausible –
Believable
Intense – *Strong*

he had emerged; but it seemed to me, accustomed as I was to his every mood, that some new possibility had dawned suddenly upon him.

It was twenty past three when we reached our terminus, and after a hasty luncheon at the buffet we pushed on at once to Scotland Yard. Holmes had already wired to Forbes, and we found him waiting to receive us -- a small, foxy man with a sharp but by no means *amiable* expression. He was decidedly *frigid* in his manner to us, especially when he heard the errand upon which we had come.

"I've heard of your methods before now, Mr. Holmes," said he, *tartly*. "You are ready enough to use all the information that the police can lay at your disposal, and then you try to finish the case yourself and bring discredit on them."

"On the contrary," said Holmes, "out of my last fifty-three cases, my name has only appeared in four, and the police have had all the credit in forty-nine. I don't blame you for not knowing this, for you are young and inexperienced, but if you wish to get on in your new duties you will work with me and not against me."

"I'd be very glad of a hint or two," said the detective, changing his manner. "I've certainly had no credit from the case so far."

"What steps have you taken?"

"Tangey, the commissionnaire, has been shadowed. He left the Guards with a good character and we can find nothing against him. His wife is a bad lot, though. I fancy she knows more about this than appears."

"Have you shadowed her?"

"We have set one of our women on to her. Mrs. Tangey drinks, and our woman has been with her twice when she was well on, but she could get nothing out of her."

"I understand that they have had brokers in the house?"

"Yes, but they were paid off."

"Where did the money come from?"

"That was all right. His pension was due. They have not shown any sign of being in funds."

"What explanation did she give of having answered the bell when Mr. Phelps rang for the coffee?" "She said that her husband was very tired and she wished to *relieve* him."

Tartly - *Sharp to the taste*
Amiable - *Friendly*
Frigid – *Cold*
Relieve – *To free, Lighten, Lessen*

"Well, certainly that would agree with his being found a little later asleep in his chair. There is nothing against them then but the woman's character. Did you ask her why she hurried away that night? Her **haste** attracted the attention of the police constable."

"She was later than usual and wanted to get home."

"Did you point out to her that you and Mr. Phelps, who started at least twenty minutes after he, got home before her?"

"She explains that by the difference between a 'bus and a hansom."

"Did she make it clear why, on reaching her house, she ran into the back kitchen?"

"Because she had the money there with which to pay off the brokers."

"She has at least an answer for everything. Did you ask her whether in leaving she met anyone or saw anyone **loitering** about Charles Street?"

"She saw no one but the constable."

"Well, you seem to have cross-examined her pretty thoroughly. What else have you done?"

"The clerk Gorot has been shadowed all these nine weeks, but without result. We can show nothing against him."

"Anything else?"

"Well, we have nothing else to go upon -- no evidence of any kind."

"Have you formed a theory about how that bell rang?"

"Well, I must **confess** that it beats me. It was a cool hand, whoever it was, to go and give the alarm like that."

"Yes, it was a queer thing to do. Many thanks to you for what you have told me. If I can put the man into your hands, you shall hear from me. Come along, Watson."

"Where are we going to now?" I asked, as we left the office.

"We are now going to interview Lord Holdhurst, the cabinet minister and future premier of England." We were fortunate in finding that Lord Holdhurst was still in his chambers in Downing Street, and on Holmes sending in his card we were instantly shown up. The statesman received us with that old-fashioned courtesy for which he is remarkable, and seated us on the two **luxuriant** lounges on either side of the

Haste – *Hurry, Rush*
Loitering – *Roaming aimlessly*
Queer - *Strange*
Luxuriant – *Lavish*

fireplace. Standing on the run between us, with his slight, tall figure, his sharp features, thoughtful face, and curling hair prematurely tinged with grey, he seemed to represent that not to common type, a nobleman who is in truth, noble.

"You name is very familiar to me, Mr. Holmes," said he, smiling. "And, of course, I cannot pretend to be ignorant of the object of your visit. There has only been one occurrence in these offices which could call for your attention. In whose interest are you acting, may I ask?"

"In that of Mr. Percy Phelps," answered Holmes.

"Ah, my unfortunate nephew! You can understand that our kinship makes it more impossible for me to screen him in any way. I fear that the incident must have a very prejudicial effect upon his career."

"But if the document is found?"

"Ah, that, of course, would be different."

"I had one or two questions which I wished to ask you, Lord Holdhurst."

"I shall be happy to give you any information in my power."

"Was it in this room that you gave your instructions as to the copying of the document?"

"It was."

"Then you could hardly have been overheard?"

"It is out of the question."

"Did you ever mention to anyone that it was your intention to give any one the treaty to be copied?" "Never." "You are certain of that?"

"Absolutely." "Well, since you never said so, and Mr. Phelps never said so, and nobody else knew anything of the matter, then the thief's presence in the room was purely accidental. He saw his chance and he took it."

The statesman smiled. "You take me out of my province there," said he.

Holmes considered for a moment. "There is another very important point which I wish to discuss with you," said he. "You feared, as I understand, that very grave results might follow from the details of this treaty becoming known."

A shadow passed over the expressive face of the statesman. "Very grave results indeed."

Noble – *Good, Aristocrat*

Ignorant – *Unaware*

Unfortunate – *Unlucky*

Prejudicial – *Detrimental, Hurtful*

"Any have they occurred?"

"Not yet."

"If the treaty had reached, let us say, the French or Russian Foreign Office, you would expect to hear of it?"

"I should," said Lord Holdhurst, with a *wry* face.

"Since nearly ten weeks have *elapsed*, then, and nothing has been heard, it is not *unfair* to suppose that for some reason the treaty has not reached them."

Lord Holdhurst shrugged his shoulders.

"We can hardly suppose, Mr. Holmes, that the thief took the treaty in order to frame it and hang it up."

"Perhaps he is waiting for a better price."

"If he waits a little longer he will get no price at all. The treaty will cease to be secret in a few months." "That is most important," said Holmes. "Of course, it is a possible supposition that the thief has had a sudden illness --"

"An attack of brain-fever, for example?" asked the statesman, flashing a swift glance at him.

"I did not say so," said Holmes, imperturbably. "And now, Lord Holdhurst, we have already taken up too much of your valuable time, and we shall wish you good day."

"Every success to your investigation, be the criminal who it may," answered the nobleman, as he bowed us out the door.

"He's a fine fellow," said Holmes, as we came out into Whitehall. "But he has a struggle to keep up his position. He is far from rich and has many calls. You noticed, of course, that his boots had been resoled. Now, Watson, I won't detain you from your legitimate work any longer. I shall do nothing more today, unless I have an answer to my cab advertisement. But I should be extremely *obliged* to you if you would come down with me to Woking tomorrow, by the same train which we took yesterday."

I met him accordingly next morning and we travelled down to Woking together. He had had no answer to his advertisement, he said, and no fresh light had been thrown upon the case. He had, when he so willed it, the utter immobility of countenance of a red Indian, and I could not gather from his appearance whether he was satisfied or not with the position of the case. His conversation, I remember, was about the Bertillon system of measurements, and he expressed his enthusiastic admiration of the French savant.

Imperturbably - *Calm and collected*
Wry – *Ironic*
Elapse – *Pass*
Unfair – *Unjust*
Oblige – *Compel, Force*

We found our client still under the charge of his devoted nurse, but looking considerably better than before. He rose from the sofa and greeted us without difficulty when we entered. "Any news?" he asked, *eagerly*.

"My report, as I expected, is a negative one," said Holmes. "I have seen Forbes, and I have seen your uncle, and I have set one or two trains of inquiry upon foot which may lead to something."

"You have not lost heart, then?"

"By no means."

"God bless you for saying that!" cried Miss Harrison. "If we keep our courage and our patience, the truth must comeout."

"We have more to tell you than you have for us," said Phelps, reseating himself upon the couch.

"I hoped you might have something."

"Yes, we have had an adventure during the night, and one which might have proved to be a serious one." His expression grew very *grave* as he spoke, and a look of something *akin* to fear sprang up in his eyes. "Do you know," said he, "that I begin to believe that I am the unconscious centre of some monstrous conspiracy, and that my life is aimed at as well as my honour?"

"Ah!" cried Holmes.

"It sounds incredible, for I have not, as far as I know, an enemy in the world. Yet from last night's experience, I can come to no other conclusion."

"Pray let me hear it."

"You must know that last night was the very first night that I have ever slept without a nurse in the room. I was so much better that I thought I could dispense with one. I had a night-light burning, however. Well, about two in the morning, I had sunk into a light sleep when I was suddenly aroused by a slight noise. It was like the sound which a mouse makes when it is gnawing a plank, and I lay listening to it for some time under the impression that it must come from that cause. Then it grew louder, and suddenly there came from the window a sharp metallic snick. I sat up in amazement. There could be no doubt what the sounds were now. The first ones had been caused by someone forcing an instrument through the slit between the *sashes*, and the second by the catch being pressed back.

Eager – *Excited*
Grave – *Serious*
Akin – *Similar*
Sashes - *Large colourful ribbons*

"There was a pause then for about ten minutes, as if the person were waiting to see whether the noise had awakened me. Then I heard a gentle creaking as the window was very slowly opened. I could stand it no longer, for my nerves are not what they used to be. I sprang out of bed and flung open the shutters. A man was crouching at the window. I could see little of him, for he was gone like a flash. He was wrapped in some sort of cloak which came across the lower part of his face. One thing only I am sure of, and that is that he had some weapon in his hand. It looked to me like a long knife. I distinctly saw the gleam of it as he turned to run."

"This is most interesting," said Holmes. "Pray what did you do then?"

"I should have followed him through the open window if I had been stronger. As it was, I rang the bell and roused the house. It took me some little time, for the bell rings in the kitchen and the servants all sleep upstairs. I shouted, however, and that brought Joseph down, and he roused the others. Joseph and the groom found marks on the bed outside the window, but the weather has been so dry lately that they found it hopeless to follow the trail across the grass. There's a place, however, on the wooden fence which skirts the road which shows signs, they tell me, as if someone had got over, and had snapped the top of the rail in doing so. I have said nothing to the local police yet, for I thought I had best have your opinion first."

This tale of our client's appeared to have an extraordinary effect upon Sherlock Holmes. He rose from his chair and paced about the room in uncontrollable excitement.

"Misfortunes never come single," said Phelps, smiling, though it was evident that his adventure had somewhat shaken him.

"You have certainly had your share," said Holmes. "Do you think you could walk round the house with me?"

"Oh, yes, I should like a little sunshine. Joseph will come, too."

"And I also," said Miss Harrison.

"I am afraid not," said Holmes, shaking his head. "I think I must ask you to remain sitting exactly where you are."

The young lady resumed her seat with an air of displeasure. Her brother, however, had joined us and we set off all

Extinct – *Died out*
Gleam – *Shimmer*
Misfortune – *Bad luck*
Displeasure – *Anger*

four together. We passed round the lawn to the outside of the young diplomatist's window. There were, as he had said, marks upon the bed, but they were hopelessly blurred and vague. Holmes stopped over them for an instant, and then rose shrugging his shoulders.

"I don't think anyone could make much of this," said he. "Let us go round the house and see why this particular room was chosen by the burglar. I should have thought those larger windows of the drawing room and dining room would have had more attractions for him."

"They are more visible from the road," suggested Mr. Joseph Harrison.

"Ah, yes, of course. There is a door here which he might have attempted. What is it for?"

"It is the side entrance for tradespeople. Of course it is locked at night."

"Have you ever had an alarm like this before?"

"Never," said our client.

"Do you keep plate in the house, or anything to attract burglars?"

"Nothing of value."

Holmes strolled round the house with his hands in his pockets and a negligent air which was unusual with him.

"By the way," said he to Joseph Harrison, "you found some place, I understand, where the fellow scaled the fence. Let us have a look at that!"

The plump young man led us to a spot where the top of one of the wooden rails had been cracked. A small fragment of the wood was hanging down. Holmes pulled it off and examined it critically.

"Do you think that was done last night? It looks rather old, does it not?"

"Well, possibly so."

"There are no marks of anyone jumping down upon the other side. No, I fancy we shall get no help here. Let us go back to the bedroom and talk the matter over."

Percy Phelps was walking very slowly, leaning upon the arm of his future brother-in-law. Holmes walked swiftly across the lawn, and we were at the open window of the bedroom long before the others came up.

Vague – *Unclear*
Negligent – *Careless*
Lean – *Bend over*
Swift – *Fast*

"Miss Harrison," said Holmes, speaking with the utmost *intensity* of manner, "you must stay where you are all day. Let nothing prevent you from staying where you are all day. It is of *utmost* importance."

"Certainly, if you wish it, Mr. Holmes," said the girl in astonishment.

"When you go to bed lock the door of this room on the outside and keep the key. Promise to do this."

"But Percy?"

"He will come to London with us."

"And am I to remain here?"

"It is for his sake. You can serve him. Quick! Promise!"

She gave a quick nod of assent just as the other two came up.

"Why do you sit moping there, Annie?" cried her brother. "Come out into the sunshine!"

"No, thank you, Joseph. I have a slight headache and this room is deliciously cool and *soothing*."

"What do you propose now, Mr. Holmes?" asked our client.

"Well, in investigating this minor affair, we must not lose sight of our main inquiry. It would be a very great help to me if you would come up to London with us."

"At once?"

"Well, as soon as you conveniently can. Say in an hour."

"I feel quite strong enough, if I can really be of any help."

"The greatest possible."

"Perhaps you would like me to stay there tonight?"

"I was just going to propose it."

"Then, if my friend of the night comes to revisit me, he will find the bird flown. We are all in your hands, Mr. Holmes, and you must tell us exactly what you would like done. Perhaps, you would prefer that Joseph came with us so as to look after me?"

"Oh, no; my friend Watson is a medical man, you know, and he'll look after you. We'll have our lunch here, if you will *permit* us, and then we shall all three set off for town together."

It was arranged as he suggested, though Miss Harrison excused herself from leaving the bedroom, in accordance with

Utmost – *Greatest, Foremost, Highest*
Intensity – *Strength*
Soothe – *Calm*
Permit – *Authorise*

Holmes's suggestion. What the object of my friend's manoeuvres was I could not *conceive*, unless it were to keep the lady away from Phelps, who, rejoiced by his returning health and by the prospect of action, lunched with us in the dining room. Holmes had still more startling surprises for us, however, for, after accompanying us down to the station and seeing us into our carriage, he calmly announced that he had no intention of leaving Woking.

"There are one or two small points which I should desire to clear up before I go," said he. "Your absence, Mr. Phelps, will in some ways rather assist me. Watson, when you reach London, you would oblige me by driving at once to Baker Street with our friend here, and remaining with him until I see you again. It is fortunate that you are old school fellows, as you must have much to talk over. Mr. Phelps can have the spare bedroom tonight, and I will be with you in time for breakfast, for there is a train which will take me into Waterloo at eight."

"But how about our investigation in London?" asked Phelps, *ruefully*.

"We can do that tomorrow. I think that just at present, I can be of more immediate use here."

"You might tell them at Briarbrae that I hope to be back tomorrow night," cried Phelps, as we began to move from the platform.

"I hardly expect to go back to Briarbrae," answered Holmes, and waved his hand to us cheerily as we shot out from the station.

Phelps and I talked it over on our journey, but neither of us could devise a satisfactory reason for this new development.

"I suppose he wants to find out some clue as to the burglary last night, if a burglar it was. For myself, I don't believe it was an ordinary thief."

"What is your own idea, then?"

"Upon my word, you may put it down to my weak nerves or not, but I believe there is some deep political *intrigue* going on around me, and that for some reason that passes my understanding, my life is aimed at by the conspirators. It sounds high-flown and absurd, but consider the facts! Why should a thief try to break in at a bedroom window, where there could be no hope of any *plunder*, and why should he come with a long knife in his hand?"

Conceive – *Believe, imagine*
Rueful – *Regretful*
Intrigue – *Conspiracy*
Plunder – *To raid, Ravage*

"You are sure it was not a house-breaker's jimmy?"

"Oh, no, it was a knife. I saw the flash of the blade quite distinctly."

"But why on earth, should you be **pursued** with such animosity?"

"Ah, that is the question."

"Well, if Holmes takes the same view, that would account for his action, would it not? Presuming that your theory is correct, if he can lay his hands upon the man who threatened you last night, he will have gone a long way towards finding who took the naval treaty. It is absurd to suppose that you have two enemies, one of whom robs you, while the other threatens your life."

"But Holmes said that he was not going to Briarbrae."

"I have known him for some time," said I, "but I never knew him do anything yet without a very good reason," and with that our conversation drifted off on to other topics.

But it was a weary day for me. Phelps was still weak after his long illness, and his misfortune made him querulous and nervous. In vain, I endeavoured to interest him in Afghanistan, in India, in social questions, in anything which might take his mind out of the groove. He would always come back to his lost treaty, wondering, guessing, **speculating**, as to what Holmes was doing, what steps Lord Holdhurst was taking, what news we should have in the morning. As the evening wore on, his excitement became quite painful.

"You have **implicit** faith in Holmes?" he asked.

"I have seen him do some remarkable things."

"But he never brought light into anything quite so dark as this?"

"Oh, yes; I have known him solve questions which presented fewer clues than yours."

"But not where such large interests are at stake?"

"I don't know that. To my certain knowledge, he has acted on behalf of three of the reigning houses of Europe in very vital matters."

"But you know him well, Watson. He is such an inscrutable fellow that I never quite know what to make of him. Do you think he is hopeful? Do you think he expects to make a success of it?"

Querulous - *Full of complaints*
Speculating - *Guessing, Suppsing, Meditation*
Pursue – *To follow, Trail, Hunt*
Animosity – *Hatred*
Implicit – *Understood*

Greatest Adventure Stories of Sherlock Holmes – 1

"He has said nothing."

"That is a bad sign."

"On the *contrary*, I have noticed that when he is off the trail, he generally says so. It is when he is on a scent and is not quite absolutely sure yet that it is the right one that he is most *taciturn*. Now, my dear fellow, we can't help matters by making ourselves nervous about them, so let me implore you to go to bed and so be fresh for whatever may await us tomorrow."

I was able at last to persuade my companion to take my advice, though I knew from his excited manner that there was not much hope of sleep for him. Indeed, his mood was infectious, for I lay tossing half the night myself, brooding over this strange problem, and inventing a hundred theories, each of which was more impossible than the last. Why had Holmes remained at Woking? Why had he asked Miss Harrison to remain in the sick room all day? Why had he been so careful not to inform the people at Briarbrae that he intended to remain near them? I *cudgelled* my brains until I fell asleep in the endeavour to find some explanation which would cover all these facts.

It was seven o'clock when I awoke, and I set off at once for Phelps's room, to find him haggard and spent after a sleepless night. His first question was whether Holmes had arrived yet.

"He'll be here when he promised," said I, "and not an instant sooner or later."

And my words were true, for shortly after eight, a hansom dashed up to the door and our friend got out of it. Standing in the window, we saw that his left hand was swathed in a bandage and that his face was very grim and pale. He entered the house, but it was some little time before he came upstairs.

"He looks like a beaten man," cried Phelps.

I was forced to *confess* that he was right. "After all," said I, "the clue of the matter lies probably here in town."

Phelps gave a groan.

"I don't know how it is," said he, "but I had hoped for so much from his return. But surely his hand was not tied up like that yesterday. What can be the matter?"

"You are not wounded, Holmes?" I asked, as my friend entered the room.

Contrary – *Opposing*
Taciturn – *Silent*
Cudgel – *Hit*
Confess – *Admit*

"Tut, it is only a scratch through my own clumsiness," he answered, nodding his good mornings to us. "This case of yours, Mr. Phelps, is certainly one of the darkest which I have ever *investigated*."

"I feared that you would find it beyond you."

"It has been a most remarkable experience."

"That bandage tells of adventures," said I. "Won't you tell us what has happened?"

"After breakfast, my dear Watson. Remember that I have breathed thirty mile of Surrey air this morning. I suppose that there has been no answer from my cabman advertisement? Well, well, we cannot expect to score every time."

The table was all laid, and just as I was about to ring, Mrs. Hudson entered wit, the tea and coffee. A few minutes later she brought in three covers, and we all drew up to the table, Holmes *ravenous*, I curious, and Phelps in the gloomiest state of depression.

"Mrs. Hudson has risen to the occasion," said Holmes, uncovering a dish of curried chicken. "Her cuisine is a little limited, but she has as good an idea of breakfast as a Scotch-woman. What have you here, Watson?"

"Ham and eggs," I answered.

"Good! What are you going to take, Mr. Phelps -- curried fowl or eggs, or will you help yourself?" "Thank you. I can eat nothing," said Phelps.

"Oh, come! Try the dish before you."

"Thank you, I would really rather not."

"Well, then," said Holmes, with a *mischievous* twinkle, "I suppose that you have no objection to helping me?"

Phelps raised the cover, and as he did so he uttered a scream, and sat there staring with a face as white as the plate upon which he looked. Across the centre of it was lying a little cylinder of blue-grey paper. He caught it up, devoured it with his eyes, and then danced madly about the room, passing it to his bosom and shrieking out in his delight. Then he fell back into an armchair so limp and exhausted with his own emotions that we had to pour brandy down his throat to keep him from fainting.

"There! there!" said Holmes, soothing, patting him upon the shoulder. "It was too bad to spring it on you like this, but

Investigate – *Look into*
Ravenous – *Very hungry*
Mischievous – *Naughty*
Shriek – *Scream*

Watson here will tell you that I never can resist a touch of the dramatic."

Phelps seized his hand and kissed it. "God bless you!" he cried. "You have saved my honour."

"Well, my own was at stake, you know," said Holmes. "I assure you it is just as hateful to me to fail in a case as it can be to you to blunder over a commission."

Phelps thrust away the precious document into the innermost pocket of his coat.

"I have not the heart to *interrupt* your breakfast any further, and yet I am dying to know how you got it and where it was."

Sherlock Holmes swallowed a cup of coffee, and turned his attention to the ham and eggs. Then he rose, lit his pipe, and settled himself down into his chair.

"I'll tell you what I did first, and how I came to do it afterwards," said he. "After leaving you at the station, I went for a charming walk through some admirable Surrey scenery to a pretty little village called Ripley, where I had my tea at an inn, and took the precaution of filling my flask and of putting a paper of sandwiches in my pocket. There I remained until evening, when I set off for Woking again, and found myself in the high-road outside Briarbrae just after sunset.

"Well, I waited until the road was clear -- it is never a very frequented one at any time, I fancy -- and then I *clambered* over the fence into the grounds."

"Surely the gate was open!" ejaculated Phelps.

"Yes, but I have a peculiar taste in these matters. I chose the place where the three fir trees stand, and behind their screen I got over without the least chance of anyone in the house being able to see me. I crouched down among the bushes on the other side, and crawled from one to the other -- witness the *disreputable* state of my trouser knees -- until I had reached the clump of rhododendrons just opposite to your bedroom window. There I squatted down and awaited developments.

"The blind was not down in your room, and I could see Miss Harrison sitting there reading by the table. It was quarter-past ten when she closed her book, fastened the shutters, and retired.

Interrupt – To *Disrupt*
Clamber – *A Climb*
Disreputable – *Infamous*

Greatest Adventure Stories of Sherlock Holmes – 1

87

"I heard her shut the door, and felt quite sure that she had turned the key in the lock."

"The key!" ejaculated Phelps.

"Yes; I had given Miss Harrison instructions to lock the door on the outside and take the key with her when she went to bed.

She carried out every one of my *injunctions* to the letter, and certainly without her cooperation you would not have that paper in you coat pocket. She **departed** then and the lights went out, and I was left squatting in the rhododendron bush.

"The night was fine, but still it was a very weary vigil. Of course, it has the sort of excitement about it that the sportsman feels when he lies beside the water course and waits for the big game.

It was very long, though -- almost as long, Watson, as when you and I waited in that deadly room when we looked into the little problem of the *Speckled Band*. There was a church clock down at Woking which struck the quarters, and I thought more than once that it had stopped.

At last, however about two in the morning, I suddenly heard the gentle sound of a bolt being pushed back and the *creaking* of a key. A moment later, the servant's door was opened, and Mr. Joseph Harrison stepped out into the moonlight."

"Joseph!" ejaculated Phelps.

"He was bareheaded, but he had a black coat thrown over his shoulder so that he could *conceal* his face in an instant if there were any alarm.

He walked on tiptoe under the shadow of the wall, and when he reached the window he worked a long-bladed knife through the sash and pushed back the catch. Then he flung open the window, and putting his knife through the crack in the shutters, he thrust the bar up and swung them open.

"From where I lay I had a perfect view of the inside of the room and of every one of his movements. He lit the two candles which stood upon the mantelpiece, and then he proceeded to turn back the corner of the carpet in the neighbourhood of the door.

Injunction – *Ban*
Creak – *Squeak*
Conceal – *Hide*

Presently, he stopped and picked out a square piece of board, such as is usually left to enable plumbers to get at the joints of the gas pipes. This one covered, as a matter of fact, the T joint which gives off the pipe which supplies the kitchen underneath.

Out of this hiding place, he drew that little cylinder of paper, pushed down the board, rearranged the carpet, blew out the candles, and walked straight into my arms as I stood waiting for him outside the window.

"Well, he has rather more *viciousness* than I gave him credit for, has Master Joseph. He flew at me with his knife, and I had to grass him twice, and got a cut over the knuckles, before I had the upper hand of him.

He looked murder out of the only eye he could see with when we had finished, but he listened to reason and gave up the papers. Having got them I let my man go, but I wired full particulars to Forbes this morning. If he is quick enough to catch his bird, well and good. But if, as I shrewdly suspect, he finds the nest empty before he gets there, why, all the better for the government.

I fancy that Lord Holdhurst for one, and Mr. Percy Phelps for another, would very much rather that the affair never got as far as a police court.

"My God!" gasped our client. "Do you tell me that during these long ten weeks of agony the stolen papers were within the very room with me all the time?"

"So it was."

"And Joseph! Joseph, a *villain* and a thief!"

"Hum! I am afraid Joseph's character is a rather deeper and more dangerous one than one might judge from his appearance. From what I have heard from him this morning,

I gather that he has lost heavily in dabbling with stocks, and that he is ready to do anything on earth to better his fortunes. Being an absolutely selfish man, when a chance presented itself, he did not allow either his sister's happiness or your *reputation* to hold his hand."

Percy Phelps sank back in his chair. "My head whirls," said he. "Your words have dazed me."

Vicious – *Cruel*
Villain – *Rouge, A wicked person*
Reputation – *Name*
Evidence – *Proof*

"The principal difficulty in your case," remarked Holmes, in his didactic fashion, "lay in the fact of there being too much *evidence*. What was vital was overlaid and hidden by what was irrelevant.

Of all the facts which were presented to us, we had to pick just those which we deemed to be essential, and then piece them together in their order, so as to reconstruct this very remarkable chain of events.

I had already begun to suspect Joseph, from the fact that you had intended to travel home with him that night, and that therefore it was a likely enough thing that he should call for you, knowing the Foreign Office well, upon his way.

When I heard that someone had been so *anxious* to get into the bedroom, in which no one but Joseph could have concealed anything -- you told us in your narrative how you had turned Joseph out when you arrived with the doctor -- my suspicions all changed to certainties, especially as the attempt was made on the first night upon which the nurse was absent, showing that the intruder was well acquainted with the ways of the house."

"How blind I have been!"

"The facts of the case, as far as I have worked them out, are these: this Joseph Harrison entered the office through the Charles Street door, and knowing his way he walked straight into your room the instant after you left it.

Finding no one there, he promptly rang the bell, and at the instant that he did so, his eyes caught the paper upon the table. A glance showed him that chance had put in his way a State document of *immense* value, and in an instant, he had thrust it into his pocket and was gone.

A few minutes *elapsed*, as you remember, before the sleepy commissionnaire drew your attention to the bell, and those were just enough to give the thief time to make his escape.

"He made his way to Woking by the first train, and having examined his booty and assured himself that it really was of immense value, he had concealed it in what he thought was a very safe place, with the intention of taking it out again in a day or two, and carrying it to the French Embassy, or

Anxious – *Nervous*
Immense – *Huge*
Elapse – *Pass by*
Baffled – *Puzzled*
Anticipate – *Expect*

wherever he thought that a long price was to be had. Then came your sudden return. He, without a moment's warning, was bundled out of his room, and from that time onward there were always at least two of you there to prevent him from regaining his treasure.

The situation to him must have been a maddening one. But at last he thought he saw his chance. He tried to steal in, but was *baffled* by your wakefulness. You remember that you did not take your usual draught that night."

"I remember."

"I fancy that he had taken steps to make that draught efficacious, and that he quite relied upon your being unconscious. Of course, I understood that he would repeat the attempt whenever it could be done with safety.

Your leaving the room gave him the chance he wanted. I kept Miss Harrison in it all day so that he might not *anticipate* us. Then, having given him the idea that the coast was clear, I kept guard as I have described.

I already knew that the papers were probably in the room, but I had no desire to rip up all the planking and skirting in search of them. I let him take them, therefore, from the hiding place, and so saved myself an **infinity** of trouble. Is there any other point which I can make clear?"

"Why did he try the window on the first occasion," I asked, "when he might have entered by the door?"

"In reaching the door, he would have to pass seven bedrooms. On the other hand, he could get out on to the lawn with ease. Anything else?"

"You do not think," asked Phelps, "that he had any murderous *intention*? The knife was only meant as a tool."

"It may be so," answered Holmes, shrugging his shoulders. "I can only say for certain that Mr. Joseph Harrison is a gentleman to whose *mercy* I should be extremely unwilling to trust."

Infinity –
Indefinitely, Timeless
Intention – *Purpose, Aim, Motive*
Mercy – *Pity*

Food For Thought

Why did Holmes want to take away Phelps from his bedroom, where a supposed burglar tried to break in with a long knife? What would have happened if Phelps would have been attacked or killed? Would he have died, or Holmes with his super-detective brain would have been able to save him?

An Understanding

Q. 1. "No, a woman's, and a woman of rare character." Who said these words and why?

Ans. _____

_____

_____

_____

_____

Q. 2. How did Sherlock Holmes perceive that Joseph Harrison was not a member of Percy Phelps's family when he met him first?

Ans. _____

_____

_____

_____

_____

Q. 3. Why was 'The Naval Treaty' so important? What would happen if the French or the Russian Embassy got hold of it?

Ans. _____

_____

_____

_____

_____

Q. 4. "Since nearly ten weeks have elapsed, then, and nothing has been heard, it is not unfair to suppose that for some reason, the treaty has not reached them." Who said these words and to whom? Where was the treaty supposed to reach?

Ans. _____

_____

_____

_____

_____

The Musgrave Ritual

~Arthur Conan Doyle

AN anomaly which often struck me in the character of my friend Sherlock Holmes was that, although in his methods of thought, he was the neatest and most methodical of mankind, and although also he affected a certain quiet primness of dress, he was nonetheless in his personal habits, one of the most untidy men that ever drove a fellow-lodger to distraction. Not that I am in the least conventional in that respect myself. The rough-and-tumble work in Afghanistan, coming on the top of a natural Bohemianism of disposition, has made me rather more *lax* than befits a medical man who keeps his cigars in the coal scuttle, his tobacco in the toe end of a Persian slipper, and his unanswered correspondence transfixed by a jack knife into the very centre of his wooden mantelpiece, then I begin to give myself virtuous airs. I have always held, too, that pistol practice should be distinctly an open-air pastime; and when Holmes, in one of his queer humours, would sit in an armchair with his hair-trigger and a hundred Boxer cartridges, and proceed to adorn the opposite wall with a patriotic V. R. Done in bullet-pocks, I felt strongly that neither the atmosphere nor the appearance of our room was improved by it.

Our chambers were always full of chemicals and of criminal relics which had a way of wandering into unlikely positions, and of turning up in the butter-dish or in even less desirable places. But his papers were my great crux. He had a horror of destroying documents, especially those which were connected with his past cases, and yet it was only once in every year or two that he would muster energy to docket and arrange them; for, as I have mentioned somewhere in these *incoherent memoirs*, the outbursts of passionate energy when he performed the remarkable feats with which his name is associated were followed by reactions of lethargy during which he would lie about with his violin and his books, hardly moving save from the sofa to the table. Thus month after month, his papers *accumulated*, until every corner of the room was stacked with bundles of manuscript which were on no account to be burned, and which could

Memoirs - *A literary, genre/Autobiography*
Relics - *Remains*
Anomaly – *Irregularity*
Lax – *Negligent*
Incoherent – *Confused*
Accumulate – *Collect*

not be put away save by their owner. One winter's night, as we sat together by the fire, I ventured to suggest to him that, as he had finished pasting extracts into his commonplace book, he might employ the next two hours in making our room a little more habitable. He could not **deny** the justice of my request, so with a rather rueful face went off to his bedroom, from which he returned presently pulling a large tin box behind him. This he placed in the middle of the floor and, squatting down upon a stool in front of it, he threw back the lid. I could see that it was already a third full of bundles of paper tied up with red tape into separate packages.

"There are enough cases here, Watson," said he, looking at me with mischievous eyes. "I think that if you knew all that I had in this box, you would ask me to pull some out instead of putting others in."

"These are the records of your early work, then?" I asked. "I have often wished that I had notes of those cases."

"Yes, my boy, these were all done prematurely before my biographer had come to **glorify** me." He lifted bundle after bundle in a tender, caressing sort of way. "They are not all successes, Watson," said he. "But there are some pretty little problems among them. Here's the record of the Tarleton Murders, and the Case of Vamberry, the Wine Merchant, and the Adventure of the old Russian Woman, and the Singular Affair of the Aluminium Crutch, as well as a full account of Ricoletti of the club-foot, and his **abominable** wife. And here -- ah, now, this really is something a little recherche."

He dived his arm down to the bottom of the chest, and brought up a small wooden box with a sliding lid, such as children's toys are kept in. From within he produced a crumpled piece of paper, and old-fashioned brass key, a peg of wood with a ball of string attached to it, and three rusty old disks of metal.

"Well, my boy, what do you make of this lot?" he asked, smiling at my expression.

"It is a curious collection."

"Very curious, and the story that hangs around it will strike you as being more curious still."

"These relics have a history then?"

"So much so that they are history."

"What do you mean by that?"

Deny – *Disagree with*
Glorify – *To honour with Praise Worship*
Abominable –
Loath some, offensive, Horrible

Sherlock Holmes picked them up one by one, and laid them along the edge of the table. Then he reseated himself in his chair and looked them over with a gleam of satisfaction in his eyes.

"These," said he, "are all that I have left to remind me of the adventure of the Musgrave Ritual."

I had heard him mention the case more than once, though I had never been able to gather the details. "I should be so glad," said I, "if you would give me an account of it."

"And leave the litter as it is?" he cried, mischievously. "Your tidiness won't bear much strain after all, Watson. But I should be glad that you should add this case to your annals, for there are points in it which make it quite *unique* in the criminal records of this or, I believe, of any other country. A collection of my trifling achievements would certainly be incomplete which contained no account of this very singular business.

"You may remember how the affair of the Gloria Scott, and my conversation with the unhappy man whose fate I told you of, first turned my attention in the direction of the profession which has become my life's work. You see me now when my name has become known far and wide, and when I am generally recognised both by the public and by the official force as being a final court of appeal in doubtful cases. Even when you knew me first, at the time of the affair which you have commemorated in 'A Study in Scarlet,' I had already established a considerable, though not a very *lucrative*, connection. You can hardly realise, then, how difficult I found it at first, and how long I had to wait before I succeeded in making any headway.

"When I first came up to London, I had rooms in Montague Street, just around the corner from the British Museum, and there I waited, filling in my too *abundant* leisure time by studying all those branches of science which might make me more efficient. Now and again cases came in my way, principally through the introduction of old fellow students, for during my last years at the University, there was a good deal of talk there about myself and my methods. The third of these cases was that of the Musgrave Ritual, and it is to the interest which was aroused by that singular chain of events, and the large issues which proved to be at stake, that I trace my first stride towards to position which I now hold.

Unique –
Extraordinary
Lucrative –
Profitable
Abundant – *Plentiful*

"Reginald Musgrave had been in the same college as myself, and I had some slight acquaintance with him. He was not generally popular among the undergraduates, though it always seemed to me that what was set down as pride was really an attempt to cover extreme natural *diffidence*. In appearance, he was a man of exceedingly aristocratic type, thin, high-nosed, and large-eyed, with languid and yet courtly manners. He was indeed a *scion* of one of the very oldest families in the kingdom, though his branch was a cadet one which had separated from the northern Musgraves some time in the sixteenth century, and had established itself in western Sussex, where the Manor House of Hurlstone is perhaps the oldest inhabited building in the county. Something of his birthplace seemed to cling to the man, and I never looked at his pale, keen face or the poise of his head without associating him with grey archways and *mullioned* windows and all the venerable wreckage of a feudal keep. Once or twice we drifted into talk, and I can remember that more than once he expressed a keen interest in my methods of observation and inference.

"For four years, I had seen nothing of him until one morning he walked into my room in Montague Street. He had changed little, was dressed like a young man of fashion -- he was always a bit of a dandy -- and preserved the same quiet, suave manner which had formerly distinguished him.

"'How has all gone with you Musgrave?" I asked, after we had cordially shaken hands.

"'You probably heard of my poor father's death,' said he; 'he was carried off about two years ago. Since then, I have of course had the Hurlstone estates to manage, and as I am member for my district as well, my life has been a busy one. But I understand, Holmes, that you are turning to practical ends those powers with which you used to amaze us?"

"'Yes,' said I, 'I have taken to living by my wits.'

"'I am delighted to hear it, for your advice at present would be exceedingly valuable to me. We have had some very strange doings at Hurlstone, and the police have been able to throw no light upon the matter. It is really the most extraordinary and *inexplicable* business.'

"You can imagine with what eagerness I listened to him, Watson, for the very chance for which I had been panting

Languid - *Lacking in vigour*

Inexplicable - *Anable to be explained*

Mullioned - *One of the radiating bars of a rose window*

Diffidence – *Shyness*

Scion – *Implant*

Suave – *Smooth*

during all those months of inaction seemed to have come within my reach. In my innermost heart, I believed that I could succeed where others failed, and now I had the opportunity to test myself.

"'Pray, let me have the details,' I cried.

"Reginald Musgrave sat down opposite to me, and lit the cigarette which I had pushed towards him.

"'You must know,' said he, 'that though I am a bachelor, I have to keep up a considerable staff of servants at Hurlstone, for it is a rambling old place, and takes a good deal of looking after. I *preserve*, too, and in the pheasant months, I usually have a house party, so that it would not do to be short-handed. Altogether there are eight maids, the cook, the butler, two footmen, and a boy. The garden and the stables, of course, have a separate staff.

"'Of these servants the one who had been longest in our service was Brunton, the butler. He was a young schoolmaster out of place when he was first taken up by my father, but he was a man of great energy and character, and he soon became quite invaluable in the household. He was a well-grown, handsome man, with a splendid forehead, and though he has been with us for twenty years, he cannot be more than forty now. With his personal advantages and his extraordinary gifts -- for he can speak several languages and play nearly every musical instrument -- it is wonderful that he should have been satisfied so long in such a position, but I suppose that he was comfortable, and lacked energy to make any change. The butler of Hurlstone is always a thing that is remembered by all who visit us.

"'But this *paragon* has one fault. He is a bit of a Don Juan, and you can imagine that for a man like him, it is not a very difficult part to play in a quiet country district. When he was married it was all right, but since he has been a widower, we have had no end of trouble with him. A few months ago, we were in hopes that he was about to settle down again for he became engaged to Rachel Howells, our second housemaid; but he has thrown her over since then and taken up with Janet Tregellis, the daughter of the head gamekeeper. Rachel -- who is a very good girl, but of an excitable Welsh *temperament* -- had a sharp touch of brain-fever, and goes about the house now -- or did until yesterday -- like a black-eyed shadow of

Preserve – *Protect*
Paragon – *Model*
Temperament –
Nature, Disposition

her former self. That was our first drama at Hurlstone; but a second one came to drive it from our minds, and it was prefaced by the *disgrace* and dismissal of butler, Brunton.

"'This was how it came about. I have said that the man was intelligent, and this very intelligence has caused his ruin, for it seems to have led to an *insatiable* curiosity about things which did not in the least concern him. I had no idea of the lengths to which this would carry him, until the merest accident opened my eyes to it.

"'I have said that the house is a rambling one. One day last week -- on Thursday night, to be more exact -- I found that I could not sleep, having foolishly taken a cup of strong cafe noir after my dinner. After struggling against it until two in the morning, I felt that it was quite hopeless, so I rose and lit the candle with the intention of continuing a novel which I was reading. The book, however, had been left in the billiard room, so I pulled on my dressing gown and started off to get it.

"'In order to reach the billiard room, I had to descend a flight of stairs and then to cross the head of a passage which led to the library and the gun room. You can imagine my surprise when, as I looked down this corridor, I saw a glimmer of light coming from the open door of the library. I had myself extinguished the lamp and closed the door before coming to bed. Naturally, my first thought was of burglars. The corridors at Hurlstone have their walls largely decorated with trophies of old weapons. From one of these, I picked a battle axe, and then, leaving my candle behind me, I crept on tiptoe down the passage and peeped in at the open door.

"'Brunton, the butler, was in the library. He was sitting, fully dressed, in an easy-chair, with a slip of paper which looked lake a map upon his knee, and his forehead sunk forward upon his hand in deep thought. I stood dumb with astonishment, watching him from the darkness. A small taper on the edge of the table shed a *feeble* light which sufficed to show me that he was fully dressed. Suddenly, as I looked, he rose from his chair, and walking over to a bureau at the side, he unlocked it and drew out one of the drawers. From this he took a paper, and returning to his seat flattened it out beside the taper on the edge of the table, and began to study it with minute attention. My *indignation* at this calm examination of our family documents overcame me so far that I took a step forward, and

Disgrace – *Shame*
Insatiable – *Greedy*
Feeble – *Weak*
Indignation –
Resentment

Brunton, looking up, saw me standing in the doorway. He sprang to his feet, his face turned livid with fear, and he thrust into his breast the chart-like paper which he had been originally studying.

"'"So!" said I. "This is how you repay the trust which we have *reposed* in you. You will leave my service tomorrow."

"'He bowed with the look of a man who is utterly crushed, and slunk past me without a word. The taper was still on the table, and by its light I glanced to see what the paper was which Brunton had taken from the bureau. To my surprise it was nothing of any importance at all, but simply a copy of the questions and answers in the singular old observance called the Musgrave Ritual. It is a sort of ceremony peculiar to our family, which each Musgrave for centuries past has gone through on his coming of age -- a thing of private interest, and perhaps of some little importance to the archaeologist, like our own *blazonings* and charges, but of no practical use whatever.'

"'We had better come back to the paper afterwards,' said I.

"'If you think it really necessary,' he answered, with some hesitation. 'To continue my statement, however: I relocked the bureau, using the key which Brunton had left, and I had turned to go when I was surprised to find that the butler had returned, and was standing before me.

"'"Mr. Musgrave, sir," he cried, in a voice which was hoarse with emotion, "I can't bear disgrace, sir. I've always been proud above my station in life, and disgrace would kill me. My blood will be on your head, sir -- it will, indeed -- if you drive me to *despair*. If you cannot keep me after what has passed, then for God's sake let me give you notice and leave in a month, as if of my own free will. I could stand that, Mr. Musgrave, but not to be cast out before all the folk that I know so well."

"'"You don't deserve much consideration, Brunton," I answered. "Your conduct has been most *infamous*. However, as you have been a long time in the family, I have no wish to bring public disgrace upon you. A month, however is too long. Take yourself away in a week, and give what reason you like for going."

"'"Only a week, sir?" he cried, in a despairing voice. "A fortnight -- say at least, a fortnight!"

Blazonings - *To describe with accurate detail*

Repose – *Relax*

Hoarse – *Rough*

Despair – *Hopelessness*

Infamous – *Notorious*

""A week," I repeated, "and you may consider yourself to have been very *leniently* dealt with."

"'He crept away, his face sunk upon his breast, like a broken man, while I put out the light and returned to my room.

""For two days after this Brunton was most *assiduous* in his attention to his duties. I made no allusion to what had passed, and waited with some curiosity to see how he would cover his disgrace. On the third morning, however, he did not appear, as was his custom, after breakfast to receive my instructions for the day. As I left the dining room, I happened to meet Rachel Howells, the maid. I have told you that she had only recently recovered from an illness, and was looking so wretchedly pale and wan that I remonstrated, with her for being at work. """You should be in bed," I said. "Come back to your duties when you are stronger."

"'She looked at me with so strange an expression that I began to suspect that her brain was affected."' "I am strong enough, Mr. Musgrave," said she.

""""We will see what the doctor says," I answered. "You must stop work now, and when you go downstairs, just say that I wish to see Brunton."

""""The butler is gone," said she.

""""Gone! Gone where?"

""""He is gone. No one has seen him. He is not in his room. Oh, yes, he is gone, he is gone!" She fell back against the wall with shriek after shriek of laughter, while I, horrified at this sudden hysterical attack, rushed to the bell to summon help. The girl was taken to her room, still screaming and sobbing, while I made inquiries about Brunton. There was no doubt about it that he had disappeared. His bed had not been slept in, he had been seen by no one since he had retired to his room the night before, and yet it was difficult to see how he could have left the house, as both the windows and doors were found to be fastened in the morning. His clothes, his watch, and even his money were in his room, but the black suit which he usually wore was missing. His slippers, too, were gone, but his boots were left behind. Where then could butler Brunton have gone in the night, and what could have become of him now?

Remonstrated – *Argued, Plead in protest*
Lenient – *Merciful, Indulgent*
Assiduous – *Diligent*
Allusion – *A passing reference*
Wan – *Pale, Gloomy*
Summon – *Call for*

"'Of course, we searched the house from cellar to garret, but there was no trace of him. It is, as I have said, a labyrinth of an old house, especially the original wing, which is now practically uninhabited; but we *ransacked* every room and cellar without discovering the least sign of the missing man. It was incredible to me that he could have gone away leaving all his property behind him, and yet where could he be? I called in the local police, but without success. Rain had fallen on the night before and we examined the lawn and the paths all round the house, but in vain. Matters were in this state, when a new development quite drew our attention away from the original mystery.

"'For two days, Rachel Howells had been so ill, sometimes *delirious*, sometimes hysterical, that a nurse had been employed to sit up with her at night. On the third night after Brunton's disappearance, the nurse, finding her patient sleeping nicely, had dropped into a nap in the armchair, when she woke in the early morning to find the bed empty, the window open, and no signs of the invalid. I was instantly aroused, and, with the two footmen, started off at once in search of the missing girl. It was not difficult to tell the direction which she had taken, for, starting from under her window, we could follow her footmarks easily across the lawn to the edge of the mere, where they vanished close to the gravel path which leads out of the grounds. The lake there is eight feet deep, and you can imagine our feelings when we saw that the trail of the poor *demented* girl came to an end at the edge of it.

"'Of course, we had the drags at once, and set to work to recover the remains, but no trace of the body could we find. On the other hand, we brought to the surface an object of a most unexpected kind. It was a linen bag which contained within it a mass of old rusted and discoloured metal and several dull-coloured pieces of pebble or glass. This strange find was all that we could get from the mere, and, although we made every possible search and inquiry yesterday, we know nothing of the fate either of Rachel Howells or of Richard Brunton. The county police are at their wits' end, and I have come up to you as a last resource.'

Demented - *Behaving irrationally*
Mere - *Lake, Pond*
Ransack – *To search throughly, Plunder*
Delirious – *Thrilled, Excited*
Endeavoured - *Attempted*
Sequence – *In an order*

"You can imagine, Watson, with what eagerness I listened to this extraordinary sequence of events, and *endeavored* to piece them together, and to devise some common thread upon which they might all hang. The butler was gone. The maid was gone. The maid had loved the butler, but had afterwards had cause to hate him. She was of Welsh blood, fiery and passionate. She had been terribly excited immediately after his disappearance. She had flung into the lake a bag containing some curious contents. These were all factors which had to be taken into consideration, and yet none of them got quite to the heart of the matter. What was the starting point of this chain of events? There lay the end of this tangled line.

"'I must see that paper, Musgrave,' said I, 'which this butler of your thought it worth his while to *consult*, even at the risk of the loss of his place.'

"'It is rather an *absurd* business, this ritual of ours,' he answered. 'But it has at least the saving grace of *antiquity* to excuse it. I have a copy of the questions and answers here if you care to run your eye over them.'

"He handed me the very paper which I have here, Watson, and this is the strange *catechism* to which each Musgrave had to submit when he came to man's estate. I will read you the questions and answers as they stand.

"'Whose was it?'

"'His who is gone.'

"'Who shall have it?'

"'He who will come.'

"'Where was the sun?'

"'Over the oak.'

"'Where was the shadow?'

"'Under the elm.'

"How was it stepped?'

"'North by ten and by ten, east by five and by five, south by two and by two, west by one and by one, and so under.'

"'What shall we give for it?'

"'All that is ours.'

"'Why should we give it?'

"'For the sake of the trust.'

Catechism - *A series of fixed questions*
Antiquity - *The ancient past*
Consult – *Seek advice from*
Absurd – *Silly and ridiculous*

"'The original has no date, but is in the spelling of the middle of the seventeenth century,' remarked Musgrave. 'I am afraid, however, that it can be of little help to you in solving this mystery.' "'At least,' said I, 'it gives us another mystery, and one which is even more interesting than the first. It may be that the solution of the one may prove to be the solution of the other. You will excuse me, Musgrave, if I say that your butler appears to me to have been a very clever man, and to have had a clearer insight than ten generations of his masters.'

"'I hardly follow you,' said Musgrave. 'The paper seems to me to be of no practical importance.'

"'But to me it seems immensely practical, and I fancy that Brunton took the same view. He had probably seen it before that night on which you caught him.'

"'It is very possible. We took no pains to hide it.'

"'He simply wished, I should imagine, to refresh his memory upon that last occasion. He had, as I understand, some sort of map or chart which he was comparing with the manuscript, and which he thrust into his pocket when you appeared.'

"'That is true. But what could he have to do with this old family custom of ours, and what does this *rigmarole* mean?'

"'I don't think that we should have much difficulty in determining that,' said I; 'with your permission we will take the first train down to Sussex, and go a little more deeply into the matter upon the spot.'

"The same afternoon saw us both at Hurlstone. Possibly you have seen pictures and read descriptions of the famous old building, so I will *confine* my account of it to saying that it is built in the shape of an L, the long arm being the more modern portion, and the shorter the ancient nucleus, from which the other had developed.

Over the low, heavily-lintelled door, in the centre of this old part, is chiselled the date, 1607, but experts agree that the beams and stone-work are really much older than this. The enormously thick walls and tiny windows of this part had in the last century driven the family into building the new wing, and the old one was used now as a storehouse and a cellar, when it was used at all. A *splendid* park with fine old

Chiselled - *Shaped or cut with a chisel*
Rigmarole - *A long, rambling story/ statement*
Confine – *Shut in*
Splendid – *Grand*

timber surrounds the house, and the lake, to which my client had referred, lay close to the avenue, about tow hundred yards from the building.

"I was already firmly convinced, Watson, that there were not three separate mysteries here, but one only, and that if I could read the Musgrave Ritual alright I should hold in my hand the clue which would lead me to the truth concerning both the butler Brunton and the maid Howells. To that then I turned all my energies. Why should this servant be so anxious to master this old formula? Evidently, because he saw something in it which had escaped all those generations of country squires, and from which he expected some personal advantage. What was it then, and how had it affected his fate?

"It was perfectly obvious to me, on reading the ritual, that the measurements must refer to some spot to which the rest of the document alluded, and that if we could find that spot, we should be in a fair way towards finding what the secret was which the old Musgraves had thought it necessary to embalm in so curious a fashion.

There were two guides given us to start with, an oak and an elm. As to the oak, there could be no question at all. Right in front of the house, upon the left-hand side of the drive, there stood a patriarch among oaks, one of the most *magnificent* trees that I have ever seen.

"'That was there when your ritual was drawn up,' said I, as we drove past it.

"'It was there at the Norman Conquest in all probability,' he answered. 'It has a *girth* of twenty-three feet.'

"'Have you any old elms?' I asked.

"'There used to be a very old one over *yonder* but it was struck by lightning ten years ago, and we cut down the stump,'

"'You can see where it used to be?'

"'Oh, yes.'

"'There are no other elms?'

"'No old ones, but plenty of beeches.'

"'I should like to see where it grew.'

Magnificent –
Splendid
Girth – *Restrain*
Yonder - *At a far distance*

"We had driven up in a dogcart, and my client led me away at once, without our entering the house, to the scar on the lawn where the elm had stood. It was nearly midway between the oak and the house. My investigation seemed to be progressing.

"'I suppose it is impossible to find out how high the elm was?' I asked.

"'I can give you it at once. It was sixty-four feet.'

"'How do you come to know it?' I asked, in surprise.

"'When my old tutor used to give me an exercise in trigonometry, it always took the shape of measuring heights. When I was a lad, I worked out every tree and building in the estate.'

"This was an *unexpected* piece of luck. My data was coming more quickly than I could have reasonably hoped.

"'Tell me,' I asked, 'did your butler ever ask you such a question?'

"Reginald Musgrave looked at me in astonishment. 'Now that you call it to my mind,' he answered, 'Brunton did ask me about the height of the tree some months ago, in connection with some little argument with the groom,'

"This was excellent news, Watson, for it showed me that I was on the right road. I looked up at the sun. It was low in the heavens, and I calculated that in less than an hour, it would lie just above the topmost branches of the old oak.

One condition mentioned in the ritual would then be fulfilled. And the shadow of the elm must mean the farther end of the shadow, otherwise the trunk would have been chosen as the guide. I had, then, to find where the far end of the shadow would fall when the sun was just clear of the oak."

"That must have been difficult, Holmes, when the elm was no longer there."

"Well, at least I knew that if Brunton could do it, I could also. Besides, there was no real difficulty. I went with Musgrave to his study and *whittled* myself this peg, to which I tied this long string with a knot at each yard.

Unexpected – *Unanticipated and surprising*
Whittle – *Carve*
Exultation – *Joy*

Then I took two lengths of a fishing-rod, which came to just six feet, and I went back with my client to where the elm had been. The sun was just grazing the top of the oak. I fastened the rod on end, marked out the direction of the shadow, and measured it. It was nine feet in length.

"Of course, the calculation now was a simple one. If a rod of six feet threw a shadow of nine, a tree of sixty-four feet would throw one of ninety-six, and the line of the one would of course be the line of the other.

I measured out the distance, which brought me almost to the wall of the house, and I thrust a peg into the spot. You can imagine my **exultation**, Watson, when within two inches of my peg, I saw a conical depression in the ground. I knew that it was the mark made by Brunton in his measurements, and that I was still upon his trail.

"From this starting point, I proceeded to step, having first taken the cardinal points by my pocket compass. Ten steps with each foot took me along parallel with the wall of the house, and again I marked my spot with a peg.

Then I carefully paced off five to the east and two to the south. It brought me to the very *threshold* of the old door. Two steps to the west meant now that I was to go two paces down the stone-flagged passage, and this was the place indicated by the ritual.

"Never have I felt such a cold chill of disappointment, Watson. For a moment is seemed to me that there must be some *radical* mistake in my calculations.

The setting sun shone full upon the passage floor, and I could see that the old, foot-worn grey stones with which it was paved were firmly cemented together, and had certainly not been moved for many a long year. Brunton had not been at work here.

I tapped upon the floor, but it sounded the same all over, and there was no sign of any crack or *crevice*. But, fortunately, Musgrave, who had begun to appreciate the meaning of my proceedings, and who was now as excited as myself, took out his manuscript to check my calculation.

"'And under,' he cried. 'You have omitted the "and under."'

Billets - *Thick pieces of wood*
Littered - *Lying about*
Threshold – *Doorstep or doorsill*
Radical – *Drastic*
Crevice – *Gap or crack*
Cravat - A stip of fabric worn around the neek

"I had thought that it meant that we were to dig, but now, of course, I saw at once that I was wrong. 'There is a cellar under this then?' I cried.

"'Yes, and as old as the house. Down here, through this door.'

"We went down a winding stone stair, and my companion, striking a match, lit a large lantern which stood on a barrel in the corner. In an instant, it was obvious that we had at last come upon the true place, and that we had not been the only people to visit the spot recently.

"It had been used for the storage of wood, but the *billets*, which had evidently been *littered* over the floor, were now piled at the sides, so as to leave a clear space in the middle. In this space, lay a large and heavy flagstone with a rusted iron ring in the centre to which a thick shepherd's-check muffler was attached.

"'By Jove!' cried my client. 'That's Brunton's muffler. I have seen it on him, and could swear to it. What has the villain been doing here?'

"At my suggestion, a couple of the county police were summoned to be present, and I then endeavoured to raise the stone by pulling on the *cravat*. I could only move it slightly, and it was with the aid of one of the constables that I succeeded at last in carrying it to one side. A black hole yawned beneath into which we all peered, while Musgrave, kneeling at the side, pushed down the lantern.

"A small chamber about seven feet deep and four feet square lay open to us. At one side of this was a *squat*, brass-bound wooden box, the lid of which was hinged upwards, with this curious old-fashioned key projecting from the lock.

"It was furred outside by a thick layer of dust, and damp and worms had eaten through the wood, so that a crop of livid fungi was growing on the inside of it. Several discs of metal, old coins apparently, such as I hold here, were scattered over the bottom of the box, but it contained nothing else.

"At the moment, however, we had no thought for the old chest, for our eyes were *riveted* upon that which crouched

Squat - *Short and thick*

Riveted - *Hold fast to*

Stagnant – *Inactive*

Countenance – *Tolerate*

Formidable – *Frightening*

Reckon – *Think*

Gauge – *Estimate*

beside it. It was the figure of a man, clad in a suit of black, who squatted down upon his hams with his forehead sunk upon the edge of the box and his two arms thrown out on each side of it.

The attitude had drawn all the **stagnant** blood to the face, and no man could have recognised that distorted liver-colored **countenance**; but his height, his dress, and his hair were all sufficient to show my client, when we had drawn the body up, that it was indeed his missing butler.

He had been dead some days, but there was no wound or bruise upon his person to show how he had met his dreadful end. When his body had been carried from the cellar, we found ourselves still confronted with a problem which was almost as **formidable** as that with which we had started.

"I confess that so far, Watson, I had been disappointed in my investigation. I had **reckoned** upon solving the matter when once I had found the place referred to in the ritual; but now I was there, and was apparently as far as ever from knowing what it was which the family had concealed with such elaborate precautions.

It is true that I had thrown a light upon the fate of Brunton, but now I had to ascertain how that fate had come upon him, and what part had been played in the matter by the woman who had disappeared. I sat down upon a keg in the corner and thought the whole matter carefully over.

"You know my methods in such cases, Watson. I put myself in the man's place and, having first gauged his intelligence, I try to imagine how I should myself have proceeded under the same circumstances.

In this case, the matter was simplified by Brunton's intelligence being quite first-rate, so that it was unnecessary to make any allowance for the personal equation, as the astronomers have dubbed it. He know that something valuable was concealed. He had spotted the place.

He found that the stone which covered it was just too heavy for a man to move unaided. What would he do next? He could not get help from outside, even if he had someone whom he could trust, without the **unbarring** of doors and

Unbarring - *To take away, to unfasten bars*
Suffice – *Be sufficient or enough*
Burly – *Heavily built*
Reconstruct – *Rebuild*

considerable risk of detection. It was better, if he could, to have his helpmate inside the house. But whom could he ask? This girl had been devoted to him.

A man always finds it hard to realise that he may have finally lost a woman's love, however badly he may have treated her. He would try by a few attentions to make his peace with the girl Howells, and then would engage her as his accomplice. Together they would come at night to the cellar, and their united force would *suffice* to raise the stone. So far I could follow their actions as if I had actually seen them.

"But for two of them, and one a woman, it must have been heavy work the raising of that stone. A *burly* Sussex policeman and I had found it no light job. What would they do to assist them?

Probably, what I should have done myself. I rose and examined carefully the different billets of wood which were scattered around the floor. Almost at once I came upon what I expected. One piece, about three feet in length, had a very marked indentation at one end, while several were flattened at the sides as if they had been compressed by some considerable weight.

Evidently, as they had dragged the stone up they had thrust the chunks of wood into the chink, until at last, when the opening was large enough to crawl through, they would hold it open by a billet placed lengthwise, which might very well become indented at the lower end, since the whole weight of the stone would press it down on to the edge of this other slab. So far I was still on safe ground.

"And now how was I to proceed to *reconstruct* this midnight drama? Clearly, only one could fit into the hole, and that one was Brunton. The girl must have waited above. Brunton then unlocked the box, handed up the contents presumably -- since they were not to be found -- and then -- and then what happened?

"What *smouldering* fire of *vengeance* had suddenly sprung into flame in this passionate Celtic woman's soul when she saw the man who had wronged her -- wronged her, perhaps, far more than we suspected -- in her power?

Blanched - *Whitened*
Vengeance – *Revenge*
Sepulcher – *Tomb or burial chamber*
Debris – *Wreckage and remains*
Lusterless – *Dull*
Smouldering - *Burn slowly with smoke*

Was it a chance that the wood had slipped, and that the stone had shut Brunton into what had become his *sepulchre*? Had she only been guilty of silence as to his fate? Or had some sudden blow from her hand dashed the support away and sent the slab crashing down into its place?

Be that as it might, I seemed to see that woman's figure still clutching at her treasure trove and flying wildly up the winding stair, with her ears ringing perhaps with the muffled screams from behind her and with the drumming of frenzied hands against the slab of stone which was choking her faithless lover's life out.

"Here was the secret of her *blanched* face, her shaken nerves, her peals of hysterical laughter on the next morning. But what had been in the box? What had she done with that? Of course, it must have been the old metal and pebbles which my client had dragged from the mere. She had thrown them in there at the first opportunity to remove the last trace of her crime.

"For twenty minutes, I had sat motionless, thinking the matter out. Musgrave still stood with a very pale face, swinging his lantern and peering down into the hole.

"'These are coins of Charles the First,' said he, holding out the few which had been in the box; 'you see we were right in fixing our date for the ritual.'

"'We may find something else of Charles the First,' I cried, as the probable meaning of the first two questions of the ritual broke suddenly upon me. 'Let me see the contents of the bag which you fished from the mere.'

"We ascended to his study, and he laid the debris before me. I could understand his regarding it as of small importance when I looked at it, for the metal was almost black and the stones lustreless and dull.

I rubbed one of them on my sleeve, however, and it glowed afterwards like a spark in the dark hollow of my hand. The metal work was in the form of a double ring, but it had been bent and twisted out of its original shape.

"'You must bear in mind,' said I, 'that the royal party made head in England even after the death of the king, and that when they at last fled they probably left many of their

Battered - *Badly damaged*
Diadem - *A jewelled crow nor headband*
Tragic – *Sad*
Relic – *Historical object*
Intrinsic - *Inherent*
Surmise – *Guess*

most precious possessions buried behind them, with the intention of returning for them in more peaceful times.'

"'My ancestor, Sir Ralph Musgrave, as a prominent Cavalier and the right-hand man of Charles the Second in his wanderings,' said my friend.

"'Ah, indeed!' I answered. 'Well now, I think that really should give us the last link that we wanted. I must congratulate you on coming into the possession, though in rather a *tragic* manner of a *relic* which is of great *intrinsic* value, but of even greater importance as an historical curiosity.'

"'What is it, then?' he gasped in astonishment.

"'It is nothing less than the ancient crown of the kings of England.'

"'The crown!'

"'Precisely. Consider what the ritual says: How does it run? "Whose was it?" "His who is gone." That was after the execution of Charles. Then, "Who shall have it?" "He who will come." That was Charles the Second, whose advent was already foreseen. There can, I think, be no doubt that this battered and shapeless diadem once encircled the brows of the royal Stuarts.'

"'And how came it in the pond?'

"'Ah, that is a question that will take some time to answer.' And with that I sketched out to him the whole long chain of *surmise* and of proof which I had constructed.

The twilight had closed in and the moon was shining brightly in the sky before my narrative was finished. "'And how was it then that Charles did not get his crown when he returned?' asked Musgrave, pushing back the relic into its linen bag.

"'Ah, there you lay your finger upon the one point which we shall probably never be able to clear up. It is likely that the Musgrave who held the secret died in the interval, and by some oversight left this guide to his descendant without explaining the meaning of it.

From that day to this, it has been handed down from father to son, until at last it came within reach of a man who tore its secret out of it and lost his life in the venture.'

Venture – *Business enterprise, An undertaking*
Retain – *Keep*

"And that's the story of the Musgrave ritual, Watson. They have the crown down at Hurlstone -- though they had some legal bother and a considerable sum to pay before they were allowed to retain it.

I am sure that if you mentioned my name they would be happy to show it to you. Of the woman nothing was ever heard, and the probability is that she got away out of England and carried herself and the memory of her crime to some land beyond the seas."

Food For Thought

"Here was the secret of her blanched face, her shaken nerves, her peals of hysterical laughter on the next morning." Who said these words and why? What would happen if Rachel Howells, the maid had not behaved in such a manner?

An Understanding

Q. 1. Who was Reginald Musgrave and how did Sherlock Holmes come across him?

Ans. _____

_____

_____

_____

_____

Q. 2. How was butler, Brunton characterwise and what were his qualities that made him indispensable in Musgrave household?

Ans. _____

_____

_____

_____

_____

Q. 3. Why was butter, Brunton dismissed from his job by Musgrave? Give a brief description of the whole incident.

Ans. _____

_____

_____

_____

_____

Q. 4. What did Rachel Howells, the poor demented maid do and how did she disappear?

Ans. _____

_____

_____

_____

_____

The Man with the Twisted Lip
~ Arthur Conan Doyle

ISa Whitney, brother of the late Elias Whitney, D.D., Principal of the Theological College of St. George's, was much addicted to opium. The habit grew upon him, as I understand, from some foolish freak when he was at college; for having read De Quincey's description of his dreams and sensations, he had drenched his tobacco with *laudanum* in an attempt to produce the same effects. He found, as so many more have done, that the practice is easier to attain than to get rid of, and for many years, he continued to be a slave to the drug, an object of *mingled* horror and pity to his friends and relatives. I can see him now, with yellow, pasty face, drooping lids, and pin-point pupils, all huddled in a chair, the wreck and ruin of a noble man.

One night -- it was in June, '89 -- there came a ring to my bell, about the hour when a man gives his first yawn and glances at the clock. I sat up in my chair, and my wife laid her needle-work down in her lap and made a little face of disappointment.

"A patient!" said she. "You'll have to go out."

I groaned, for I had newly come back from a weary day.

We heard the door open, a few hurried words, and then quick steps upon the *linoleum*. Our own door flew open, and a lady, clad in some dark-colored stuff, with a black veil, entered the room.

"You will excuse my calling so late," she began, and then, suddenly losing her self-control, she ran forward, threw her arms about my wife's neck, and sobbed upon her shoulder. "Oh, I'm in such trouble!" she cried; "I do so want a little help."

"Why," said my wife, pulling up her veil, "it is Kate Whitney. How you startled me, Kate! I had not an idea who you were when you came in."

"I didn't know what to do, so l came straight to you." That was always the way. Folk, who were in *grief* came to my wife like birds to a lighthouse.

"It was very sweet of you to come. Now, you must have some wine and water, and sit here comfortably and tell us all about it. Or should you rather that I sent James off to bed?"

Laudanum - *A tincture of opium*
Linoleum - *A durable, washable material*
Mingle – *Mix*
Drooping - *Bend or hang downwards*
Grief – *Sorrow*

"Oh, no, no! I want the doctor's advice and help, too. It's about Isa. He has not been home for two days. I am so frightened about him!"

It was not the first time that she had spoken to us of her husband's trouble, to me as a doctor, to my wife as an old friend and school companion. We *soothed* and comforted her by such words as we could find. Did she know where her husband was? Was it possible that we could bring him back to her?

It seems that it was. She had the surest information that of late he had, when the fit was on him, made use of an opium den in the farthest east of the City. Hitherto his *orgies* had always been confined to one day, and he had come back, twitching and shattered, in the evening. But now the spell had been upon him eight-and-forty hours, and he lay there, doubtless among the *dregs* of the docks, breathing in the poison or sleeping off the effects. There he was to be found, she was sure of it, at the Bar of Gold, in Upper Swandam Lane. But what was she to do? How could she, a young and *timid* woman, make her way into such a place and pluck her husband out from among the ruffians who surrounded him?

There was the case, and of course there was but one way out of it. Might I not escort her to this place? And then, as a second thought, why should she come at all? I was Isa Whitney's medical adviser, and as such, I had influence over him. I could manage it better if I were alone. I promised her on my word that I would send him home in a cab within two hours if he were indeed at the address which she had given me. And so in ten minutes, I had left my armchair and cheery sitting room behind me, and was speeding eastward in a hansom on a strange *errand*, as it seemed to me at the time, though the future only could show how strange it was to be.

But there was no great difficulty in the first stage of my adventure. Upper Swandam Lane is a *vile* alley lurking behind the high wharves which line the north side of the river to the east of London Bridge. Between a slop-shop and a gin-shop, approached by a steep flight of steps leading down to a black gap like the mouth of a cave, I found the den of which I was in search. Ordering my cab to wait, I passed down the steps, worn hollow in the centre by the ceaseless tread of drunken feet; and by the light of a flickering oil-lamp above the door I found the latch and made my way into a long, low room, thick

Greatest Adventure Stories of Sherlock Holmes – 1

and heavy with the brown opium smoke, and terraced with wooden berths, like the forecastle of an emigrant ship.

Through the gloom, one could dimly catch a glimpse of bodies lying in strange fantastic poses, bowed shoulders, bent knees, heads thrown back, and chins pointing upward, with here and there a dark, lack-lustre eye turned upon the new-comer. Out of the black shadows, there glimmered little red circles of light, now bright, now faint, as the burning poison waxed or waned in the bowls of the metal pipes. The most lay silent, but some muttered to themselves, and others talked to-gether in a strange, low, *monotonous* voice, their conversation coming in gushes, and then suddenly tailing off into silence, each mumbling out his own thoughts and paying little heed to the words of his neighbour. At the farther end was a small brazier of burning charcoal, beside which on a three-legged wooden stool, there sat a tall, thin old man, with his jaw resting upon his two fists, and his elbows upon his knees, staring into the fire.

As I entered, a sallow Malay attendant had hurried up with a pipe for me and a supply of the drug, *beckoning* me to an empty berth.

"Thank you. I have not come to stay," said I. "There is a friend of mine here, Mr. Isa Whitney, and I wish to speak with him."

There was a movement and an exclamation from my right, and peering through the gloom I saw Whitney, pale, *haggard*, and *unkempt*, staring out at me.

"My God! It's Watson," said he. He was in a pitiable state of reaction, with every nerve in a twitter. "I say, Watson, what o'clock is it?"

"Nearly eleven."

"Of what day?"

"Of Friday, June 19th."

"Good heavens! I thought it was Wednesday. It is Wednesday. What d'you want to frighten the chap for?" He sank his face onto his arms and began to sob in a high *treble* key.

"I tell you that it is Friday, man. Your wife has been waiting these two days for you. You should be ashamed of yourself!"

"So I am. But you've got mixed, Watson, for I have only been here a few hours, three pipes, four pipes -- I forget how

High - *Pitched*
Brazier - *One, who makes brass articles*
Monotonous – *Dull and boring*
Beckon – *Summon*
Haggard – *Tired, Exhausted*
Unkempt – *Untidy*

many. But I'll go home with you. I wouldn't frighten Kate -- poor little Kate. Give me your hand! Have you a cab?"

"Yes, I have one waiting."

"Then I shall go in it. But I must owe something. Find what I owe, Watson. I am all off *colour*. I can do nothing for myself."

I walked down the narrow passage between the double row of sleepers, holding my breath to keep out the vile, stupefying fumes of the drug, and looking about for the manager. As I passed the tall man, who sat by the brazier, I felt a sudden pluck at my skirt, and a low voice whispered, "Walk past me, and then look back at me." The words fell quite distinctly upon my ear. I glanced down. They could only have come from the old man at my side, and yet he sat now as absorbed as ever, very thin, very wrinkled, bent with age, an opium pipe dangling down from between his knees, as though it had dropped in sheer *lassitude* from his fingers. I took two steps forward and looked back. It took all my self-control to prevent me from breaking out into a cry of astonishment. He had turned his back so that none could see him but I. His form had filled out, his wrinkles were gone, the dull eyes had regained their fire, and there, sitting by the fire and grinning at my surprise, was none other than Sherlock Holmes. He made a slight motion to me to approach him, and instantly, as he turned his face half around to the company once more, subsided into a *doddering*, loose-lipped senility.

"Holmes!" I whispered, "what on earth are you doing in this den?"

"As low as you can," he answered; "I have excellent ears. If you would have the great kindness to get rid of that Sottish friend of yours, I should be exceedingly glad to have a little talk with you."

"I have a cab outside."

"Then pray send him home in it. You may safely trust him, for he appears to be too limp to get into any *mischief*. I should recommend you also to send a note by the cabman to your wife to say that you have thrown in your lot with me. If you will wait outside, I shall be with you in five minutes."

It was difficult to refuse any of Sherlock Holmes's requests, for they were always so exceedingly definite, and put forward with such a quiet air of mastery. I felt, however, that

Lassitude –
Tiredness memory loss
Senility - *Exhibiting*
Doddering – *Foolish*
Mischief –
Misbehaviour

when Whitney was once confined in the cab my mission was practically accomplished; and for the rest, I could not wish anything better than to be associated with my friend in one of those singular adventures which were the normal condition of his existence. In a few minutes, I had written my note, paid Whitney's bill, led him out to the cab, and seen him driven through the darkness. In a very short time, a *decrepit* figure had emerged from the opium den, and I was walking down the street with Sherlock Holmes. For two streets, he shuffled along with a bent back and an uncertain foot. Then, glancing quickly around, he straightened himself out and burst into a hearty fit of laughter.

"I suppose, Watson," said he, "that you imagine that I have added opium-smoking to cocaine injections, and all the other little weaknesses on which you have *favoured* me with your medical views."

"I was certainly surprised to find you there."

"But not more so than I to find you."

"I came to find a friend."

"And I to find an enemy."

"An enemy?"

"Yes; one of my natural enemies, or, shall I say, my natural prey. Briefly, Watson, I am in the midst of a very remarkable inquiry, and I have hoped to find a clue in the *incoherent* ramblings of these sots, as I have done before now. Had I been recognised in that den, my life would not have been worth an hour's purchase; for I have used it before now for my own purposes, and the rascally Lascar who runs it has sworn to have vengeance upon me. There is a trap-door at the back of that building, near the corner of Paul's Wharf, which could tell some strange tales of what has passed through it upon the moonless nights."

"What! You do not mean bodies?"

"Ay, bodies, Watson. We should be rich men if we had 1000 pounds for every poor devil who has been done to death in that den. It is the vilest murder-trap on the whole riverside, and I fear that Neville St. Clair has entered it never to leave it more. But our trap should be here." He put his two forefingers between his teeth and whistled shrilly -- a signal which was answered by a similar whistle from the distance, followed shortly by the rattle of wheels and the clink of horses' hoofs.

Shuffled - *Slide along the floor while walking*
Decrepit – *Old*
Incoherent – *Confused, Irrational*

"Now, Watson," said Holmes, as a tall dog-cart dashed up through the gloom, throwing out two golden tunnels of yellow light from its side lanterns. "You'll come with me, won't you?

"If I can be of use."

"Oh, a trusty comrade is always of use; and a chronicler still more so. My room at The Cedars is a double-bedded one."

"The Cedars?"

"Yes; that is Mr. St. Clair's house. I am staying there while I conduct the inquiry."

"Where is it, then?"

"Near Lee, in Kent. We have a seven-mile drive before us."

"But I am all in the dark."

"Of course, you are. You'll know all about it presently. Jump up here. All right, John; we shall not need you. Here's half a crown. Look out for me tomorrow, about eleven. Give her her head. So long, then!"

He flicked the horse with his whip, and we dashed away through the endless succession of sombre and deserted streets, which widened gradually, until we were flying across a broad **balustraded** bridge, with the **murky** river flowing **sluggishly** beneath us. Beyond lay another dull **wilderness** of bricks and mortar, its silence broken only by the heavy, regular footfall of the policeman, or the songs and shouts of some belated party of revellers. A dull wrack was drifting slowly across the sky, and a star or two twinkled dimly here and there through the rifts of the clouds. Holmes drove in silence, with his head sunk upon his breast, and the air of a man who is lost in thought, while I sat beside him, curious to learn what this new quest might be which seemed to tax his powers so sorely, and yet afraid to break in upon the current of his thoughts. We had driven several miles, and were beginning to get to the fringe of the belt of suburban villas, when he shook himself, shrugged his shoulders, and lit up his pipe with the air of a man who has satisfied himself that he is acting for the best.

Sluggishly - *Lacking alertness*
Wilderness - *A large wild tract of land*
Balustrade – *Barrier*
Murky – *Foggy and dark*

"You have a grand gift of silence, Watson," said he. "It makes you quite invaluable as a companion. 'Pon my word, it is a great thing for me to have someone to talk to, for my own thoughts are not overpleasant. I was wondering what I should say to this dear little woman tonight when she meets me at the door."

"You forget that I know nothing about it."

"I shall just have time to tell you the facts of the case before we get to Lee. It seems *absurdly* simple, and yet, somehow I can get nothing to go upon. There's plenty of thread, no doubt, but I can't get the end of it into my hand. Now, I'll state the case clearly and concisely to you, Watson, and maybe you can see a spark where all is dark to me."

"Proceed, then."

"Some years ago -- to be definite, in May, 1884 -- there came to Lee a gentleman, Neville St. Clair by name, who appeared to have plenty of money. He took a large villa, laid out the grounds very nicely, and lived generally in good style. By degrees, he made friends in the neighbourhood, and in 1887, he married the daughter of a local brewer, by whom he now has two children. He had no *occupation*, but was interested in several companies and went into town as a rule in the morning, returning by the 5:14 from Cannon Street every night. Mr. St. Clair is now thirty-seven years of age, is a man of *temperate* habits, a good husband, a very affectionate father, and a man who is popular with all who know him. I may add that his whole debts at the present moment, as far as we have been able to *ascertain* amount to 88 pounds 10s., while he has 220 pounds standing to his credit in the Capital and Counties Bank. There is no reason, therefore, to think that money troubles have been weighing upon his mind.

"Last Monday, Mr. Neville St. Clair went into town rather earlier than usual, remarking before he started that he had two important commissions to perform, and that he would bring his little boy home a box of bricks. Now, by the merest chance, his wife received a telegram upon this same Monday, very shortly after his departure, to the effect that a small parcel of considerable value which she had been expecting was waiting for her at the offices of the Aberdeen Shipping Company. Now, if you are well up in London, you will know that the office of the company is in Fresno Street, which branches out of Upper Swandam Lane, where you found me tonight. Mrs. St. Clair had her lunch, started for the City, did some shopping, proceeded to the company's office, got her packet, and found herself at exactly 4:35 walking through Swandam Lane on her way back to the station. Have you followed me so far?"

"It is very clear."

Absurd – *Silly*
Occupation – *Job*
Temperate – *Mild*
Ascertain –
Determine

"If you remember, Monday was an exceedingly hot day, and Mrs. St. Clair walked slowly, glancing about in the hope of seeing a cab, as she did not like the neighbourhood in which she found herself. While she was walking in this way down Swandam Lane, she suddenly heard an ejaculation or cry, and was struck cold to see her husband looking down at her and, as it seemed to her, **beckoning** to her from a second-floor window. The window was open, and she distinctly saw his face, which she describes as being terribly **agitated**. He waved his hands frantically to her, and then vanished from the window so suddenly that it seemed to her that he had been plucked back by some **irresistible** force from behind. One singular point which struck her quick feminine eye was that although he wore some dark coat, such as he had started to town in, he had on neither collar nor necktie.

"Convinced that something was **amiss** with him, she rushed down the steps -- for the house was none other than the opium den in which you found me tonight -- and running through the front room, she attempted to ascend the stairs which led to the first floor. At the foot of the stairs, however, she met this Lascar scoundrel of whom I have spoken, who thrust her back and, aided by a Dane, who acts as assistant there, pushed her out into the street. Filled with the most maddening doubts and fears, she rushed down the lane and, by rare good-fortune, met in Fresno Street, a number of constables with an inspector, all on their way to their beat. The inspector and two men accompanied her back, and in spite of the continued resistance of the proprietor, they made their way to the room in which Mr. St. Clair had last been seen. There was no sign of him there. In fact, in the whole of that floor, there was no one to be found save a crippled wretch of hideous aspect, who, it seems, made his home there. Both he and the Lascar stoutly swore that no one else had been in the front room during the afternoon. So determined was their denial that the inspector was staggered, and had almost come to believe that Mrs. St. Clair had been **deluded** when, with a cry, she sprang at a small deal box which lay upon the table and tore the lid from it. Out there fell a cascade of children's bricks. It was the toy which he had promised to bring home.

Beckoning - *To signal, summon*
Agitate – *Disturb*
Irresistible – *Tempting*
Amiss – *Wrong*
Delude – *Cheat*

"This discovery, and the evident confusion which the cripple showed, made the inspector realise that the matter was serious. The rooms were carefully examined, and results all pointed to an *abominable* crime. The front room was plainly furnished as a sitting room and led into a small bedroom, which looked out upon the back of one of the *wharves*. Between the *wharf* and the bedroom window, is a narrow strip, which is dry at low tide but is covered at high tide with at least four and a half feet of water. The bedroom window was a broad one and opened from below. On examination traces of blood were to be seen upon the windowsill, and several scattered drops were visible upon the wooden floor of the bedroom. Thrust away behind a curtain in the front room were all the clothes of Mr. Neville St. Clair, with the exception of his coat. His boots, his socks, his hat, and his watch -- all were there. There were no signs of violence upon any of these garments, and there were no other traces of Mr. Neville St. Clair. Out of the window, he must apparently have gone for no other exit could be discovered, and the *ominous* bloodstains upon the *sill* gave little promise that he could save himself by swimming, for the tide was at its very highest at the moment of the tragedy.

"And now as to the villains who seemed to be immediately implicated in the matter. The Lascar was known to be a man of the *vilest antecedents*, but as, by Mrs. St. Clair's story, he was known to have been at the foot of the stair within a very few seconds of her husband's appearance at the window, he could hardly have been more than an accessory to the crime. His defensce was one of absolute ignorance, and he protested that he had no knowledge as to the doings of Hugh Boone, his lodger, and that he could not account in any way for the presence of the missing gentleman's clothes.

"So much for the Lascar manager. Now for the sinister cripple who lives upon the second floor of the opium den, and who was certainly the last human being whose eyes rested upon Neville St. Clair. His name is Hugh Boone, and his *hideous* face is one which is familiar to every man who goes much to the City. He is a professional beggar, though in order to avoid the police regulations he pretends to run a small trade in wax *vestas*. Some little distance down Threadneedle Street,

Abominable - *Detestable*
Sinister - *Bad, evil*
Wharf – *quay*
Ominous – *Threatening*
Antecedent – *Precursor*
Hideous – *Ugly*

upon the left-hand side, there is, as you may have remarked, a small angle in the wall. Here it is that this creature takes his daily seat, cross-legged with his tiny stock of matches on his lap, and as he is a piteous spectacle, a small rain of charity descends into the greasy leather cap which lies upon the pavement beside him. I have watched the fellow more than once before ever I thought of making his professional acquaintance, and I have been surprised at the harvest which he has reaped in a short time.

His appearance, you see, is so remarkable that no one can pass him without observing him. A shock of orange hair, a pale face disfigured by a horrible scar, which, by its contraction, has turned up the outer edge of his upper lip, a bulldog chin, and a pair of very penetrating dark eyes, which present a singular contrast to the colour of his hair, all mark him out from amid the common crowd of *mendicants* and so, too, does his wit, for he is ever ready with a reply to any piece of *chaff* which may be thrown at him by the *passers* by.

This is the man whom we now learn to have been the lodger at the opium den, and to have been the last man to see the gentleman of whom we are in quest."

"But a cripple!" said I. "What could he have done single-handed against a man in the prime of life?" "He is a cripple in the sense that he walks with a limp; but in other respects, he appears to be a powerful and well-nurtured man. Surely your medical experience would tell you, Watson, that weakness in one limb is often compensated for by exceptional strength in the others."

"Pray continue your narrative."

"Mrs. St. Clair had fainted at the sight of the blood upon the window, and she was escorted home in a cab by the police, as her presence could be of no help to them in their investigations. Inspector Barton, who had charge of the case, made a very careful examination of the premises, but without finding anything which threw any light upon the matter.

One mistake had been made in not arresting Boone instantly, as he was allowed some few minutes during which he might have communicated with his friend Lascar, but this

Mendicant – *Beggar*
Seize – *Grab*
Incriminate –
Implicate, *To accuse*
Strenuous – *Tiring*

fault was soon remedied, and he was seized and searched, without anything being found which could *incriminate* him.

There were, it is true, some blood stains upon his right shirt-sleeve, but he pointed to his ring finger, which had been cut near the nail, and explained that the bleeding came from there, adding that he had been to the window not long before, and that the stains which had been observed there came doubtless from the same source. He denied *strenuously* having ever seen Mr. Neville St. Clair and swore that the presence of the clothes in his room was as much a mystery to him as to the police. As to Mrs. St. Clair's assertion that she had actually seen her husband at the window, he declared that she must have been either mad or dreaming.

He was removed, loudly protesting, to the police-station, while the inspector remained upon the premises in the hope that the *ebbing* tide might afford some fresh clue.

"And it did, though they hardly found upon the mud-bank what they had feared to find. It was Neville St. Clair's coat, and not Neville St. Clair, which lay uncovered as the tide receded. And what do you think they found in the pockets?"

"I cannot imagine."

"No, I don't think you would guess. Every pocket stuffed with pennies and half-pennies -- 421 pennies and 270 half-pennies. It was no wonder that it had not been swept away by the tide. But a human body is a different matter. There is a fierce *eddy* between the wharf and the house.

It seemed likely enough that the weighted coat had remained when the stripped body had been sucked away into the river."

"But I understand that all the other clothes were found in the room. Would the body be dressed in a coat alone?"

"No, sir, but the facts might be met speciously enough. Suppose that this man Boone had thrust Neville St. Clair through the window, there is no human eye which could have seen the deed. What would he do then?

It would of course instantly strike him that he must get rid of the tell-tale garments. He would seize the coat, then, and be in the act of throwing it out, when it would occur to him that it would swim and not sink.

Eddy - *A small whirlpool*
Assert – *Declare*
Ebb – *Recede*
Scuffle – *Fight, Tussle*
Feasible – *Possible*

He has little time, for he has heard the *scuffle* downstairs when the wife tried to force her way up, and perhaps, he has already heard from his Lascar confederate that the police are hurrying up the street. There is not an instant to be lost.

He rushes to some secret hoard, where he has accumulated the fruits of his beggary, and he stuffs all the coins upon which he can lay his hands into the pockets to make sure of the coat's sinking. He throws it out, and would have done the same with the other garments had not he heard the rush of steps below, and only just had time to close the window when the police appeared."

"It certainly sounds *feasible*."

"Well, we will take it as a working hypothesis for want of a better. Boone, as I have told you, was arrested and taken to the station, but it could not be shown that there had ever before been anything against him.

He had for years been known as a professional beggar, but his life appeared to have been a very quiet and innocent one. There the matter stands at present, and the questions which have to be solved -- what Neville St. Clair was doing in the opium den, what happened to him when there, where is he now, and what Hugh Boone had to do with his disappearance -- are all as far from a solution as ever.

I confess that I cannot recall any case within my experience which looked at the first glance so simple and yet which presented such difficulties." While Sherlock Holmes had been detailing this singular series of events, we had been whirling through the outskirts of the great town until the last *straggling* houses had been left behind, and we rattled along with a country hedge upon either side of us.

Just as he finished, however, we drove through two scattered villages, where a few lights still glimmered in the windows.

"We are on the outskirts of Lee," said my companion. "We have touched on three English counties in our short drive, starting in Middlesex, passing over an angle of Surrey, and ending in Kent. See that light among the trees?

Straggling - *To wander about*
Confess – *Admit*
Whirl – *Spin*
Clink - *To make or cause a light, sharp ringing sound*

That is The Cedars, and beside that lamp sits a woman whose anxious ears have already, I have little doubt, caught the clink of our horse's feet."

"But why are you not conducting the case from Baker Street?" I asked.

"Because there are many inquiries which must be made out here. Mrs. St. Clair has most kindly put two rooms at my disposal, and you may rest assured that she will have nothing but a welcome for my friend and colleague. I hate to meet her, Watson, when I have no news of her husband. Here we are. Whoa, there, whoa!"

We had pulled up in front of a large villa which stood within its own grounds. A stable-boy had run out to the horse's head, and springing down, I followed Holmes up the small, winding gravel-drive which led to the house. As we approached, the door flew open, and a little blonde woman stood in the opening, clad in some sort of light mousseline de soie, with a touch of fluffy pink chiffon at her neck and wrists.

She stood with her figure outlined against the flood of light, one hand upon the door, one half-raised in her eagerness, her body slightly bent, her head and face protruded, with eager eyes and parted lips, a standing question.

"Well?" she cried, "well?" And then, seeing that there were two of us, she gave a cry of hope which sank into a groan as she saw that my companion shook his head and shrugged his shoulders. "No good news?"

"None." "No bad?"

"No." "Thank God for that. But come in. You must be weary, for you have had a long day."

"This is my friend, Dr. Watson. He has been of most vital use to me in several of my cases, and a lucky chance has made it possible for me to bring him out and associate him with this investigation." "I am *delighted* to see you," said she, pressing my hand warmly. "You will, I am sure, forgive anything that may be wanting in our arrangements, when you consider the blow which has come so suddenly upon us."

"My dear madam," said I, "I am an old campaigner, and if I were not I can very well see that no apology is needed. If

Weary – *Tired*
Hysterical - *Very emotional outbreak*
Delighted – *Pleased*
Sprang – *Jump*
Galvanise – *Spur*

I can be of any assistance, either to you or to my friend here, I shall be indeed happy."

"Now, Mr. Sherlock Holmes," said the lady as we entered a well-lit dining room, upon the table of which a cold supper had been laid out, "I should very much like to ask you one or two plain questions, to which I beg that you will give a plain answer."

"Certainly, madam."

"Do not trouble about my feelings. I am not *hysterical*, nor given to fainting. I simply wish to hear your real, real opinion."

"Upon what point?"

"In your heart of hearts, do you think that Neville is alive?"

Sherlock Holmes seemed to be embarrassed by the question. "Frankly, now!" she repeated, standing upon the rug and looking keenly down at him as he leaned back in a basket chair.

"Frankly, then, madam, I do not."

"You think that he is dead?"

"I do."

"Murdered?" "I don't say that. Perhaps."

"And on what day did he meet his death?"

"On Monday."

"Then perhaps, Mr. Holmes, you will be good enough to explain how it is that I have received a letter from him today."

Sherlock Holmes sprang out of his chair as if he had been galvanised.

"What!" he roared.

"Yes, today." She stood smiling, holding up a little slip of paper in the air.

"May I see it?"

"Certainly." He snatched it from her in his eagerness, and smoothing it out upon the table he drew over the lamp and examined it *intently*. I had left my chair and was gazing at it over his shoulder. The envelope was a very coarse one and was stamped with the Gravesend postmark and with the date of that very day, or rather of the day before, for it was considerably after midnight.

"Coarse writing," murmured Holmes. "Surely this is not your husband's writing, madam."

Trifle - *A thing of very little value*
Intent – *Intention*
Perceive – *Distinguish*
Rectify – *Correct*

"No, but the enclosure is."

"I *perceive* also that whoever addressed the envelope had to go and inquire as to the address."

"How can you tell that?"

"The name, you see, is in perfectly black ink, which has dried itself. The rest is of the greyish colour, which shows that blotting-paper has been used. If it had been written straight off, and then blotted, none would be of a deep black shade.

This man has written the name, and there has then been a pause before he wrote the address, which can only mean that he was not familiar with it. It is, of course, a trifle, but there is nothing so important as trifles. Let us now see the letter. Ha! there has been an enclosure here!"

"Yes, there was a ring. His signet ring."

"And you are sure that this is your husband's hand?"

"One of his hands."

"One?" "His hand when he wrote hurriedly. It is very unlike his usual writing, and yet I know it well."

"'Dearest do not be frightened. All will come well. There is a huge error which may take some little time to *rectify*. Wait in patience. -- NEVILLE.' Written in pencil upon the fly-leaf of a book, octavo size, no watermark. Hum!

Posted today in Gravesend by a man with a dirty thumb. Ha! And the flap has been gummed, if I am not very much in error, by a person who had been chewing tobacco. And you have no doubt that it is your husband's hand, madam?"

"None. Neville wrote those words."

"And they were posted today at Gravesend. Well, Mrs. St. Clair, the clouds lighten, though I should not *venture* to say that the danger is over."

"But he must be alive, Mr. Holmes."

"Unless this is a clever *forgery* to put us on the wrong scent. The ring, after all, proves nothing. It may have been taken from him. '

"No, no; it is, it is his very own writing!"

"Very well. It may, however, have been written on Monday and only posted today."

"That is possible."

Forgery – *Fake, False*
Corroborate – *Confirm*
Inarticulate – *Lacking the ability to express*

"If so, much may have happened between."

"Oh, you must not discourage me, Mr. Holmes. I know that all is well with him. There is so keen a sympathy between us that I should know if evil came upon him.

On the very day that I saw him last, he cut himself in the bedroom, and yet I in the dining room rushed upstairs instantly with the utmost certainty that something had happened. Do you think that I would respond to such a trifle and yet be ignorant of his death?"

"I have seen too much not to know that the impression of a woman may be more valuable than the conclusion of an analytical reasoner. And in this letter you certainly have a very strong piece of evidence to *corroborate* your view. But if your husband is alive and able to write letters, why should he remain away from you?"

"I cannot imagine. It is unthinkable."

"And on Monday, he made no remarks before leaving you?"

"No." "And you were surprised to see him in Swandam Lane?"

"Very much so."

"Was the window open?"

"Yes." "Then he might have called to you?"

"He might."

"He only, as I understand, gave an *inarticulate* cry?"

"Yes." "A call for help, you thought?"

"Yes. He waved his hands."

"But it might have been a cry of surprise. Astonishment at the unexpected sight of you might cause him to throw up his hands?"

"It is possible."

"And you thought he was pulled back?"

"He disappeared so suddenly."

"He might have leaped back. You did not see anyone else in the room?"

"No, but this horrible man confessed to having been there, and the Lascar was at the foot of the stairs."

Disposal – *Removal*
Fathom – *Understand*
Aquiline – *Hooked*

"Quite so. Your husband, as far as you could see, had his ordinary clothes on?"

"But without his collar or tie. I distinctly saw his bare throat."

"Had he ever spoken of Swandam Lane?"

"Never." "Had he ever showed any signs of having taken opium?"

"Never." "Thank you, Mrs. St. Clair. Those are the principal points about which I wished to be absolutely clear. We shall now have a little supper and then retire, for we may have a very busy day tomorrow."

A large and comfortable double-bedded room had been placed at our *disposal*, and I was quickly between the sheets, for I was weary after my night of adventure.

Sherlock Holmes was a man, however, who, when he had an unsolved problem upon his mind, would go for days, and even for a week, without rest, turning it over, rearranging his facts, looking at it from every point of view until he had either *fathomed* it or convinced himself that his data were insufficient. It was soon evident to me that he was now preparing for an all-night sitting. He took off his coat and waistcoat, put on a large blue dressing-gown, and then wandered about the room collecting pillows from his bed and cushions from the sofa and armchairs.

With these, he constructed a sort of Eastern divan, upon which he perched himself cross-legged, with an ounce of shag tobacco and a box of matches laid out in front of him. In the dim light of the lamp I saw him sitting there, an old briar pipe between his lips, his eyes fixed vacantly upon the corner of the ceiling, the blue smoke curling up from him, silent, motionless, with the light shining upon his strong-set *aquiline* features.

So he sat as I dropped off to sleep, and so he sat when a sudden ejaculation caused me to wake up, and I found the summer sun shining into the apartment.

The pipe was still between his lips, the smoke still curled upward, and the room was full of a dense tobacco haze, but nothing remained of the heap of *shag* which I had seen upon the previous night.

"Awake, Watson?" he asked.

"Yes." "Game for a morning drive?"

Shag - *A mass of rough, matted hair or wool*
Sombre - *Very serious*
Chuckle – *Giggle*
Incredulity – *Disbelief*

"Certainly." "Then dress. No one is stirring yet, but I know where the stable boy sleeps, and we shall soon have the trap out." He **chuckled** to himself as he spoke, his eyes twinkled, and he seemed a different man to the sombre thinker of the previous night.

As I dressed, I glanced at my watch. It was no wonder that no one was stirring. It was twenty-five minutes past four. I had hardly finished when Holmes returned with the news that the boy was putting in the horse.

"I want to test a little theory of mine," said he, pulling on his boots. "I think, Watson, that you are now standing in the presence of one of the most absolute fools in Europe. I deserve to be kicked from here to Charing Cross. But I think I have the key of the affair now."

"And where is it?" I asked, smiling.

"In the bathroom," he answered. "Oh, yes, I am not joking," he continued, seeing my look of **incredulity**. "I have just been there, and I have taken it out, and I have got it in this Gladstone bag. Come on, my boy, and we shall see whether it will not fit the lock."

We made our way downstairs as quietly as possible, and out into the bright morning sunshine. In the road stood our horse and trap, with the half-clad stable boy waiting at the head. We both sprang in, and away we dashed down the London Road.

A few country carts were stirring, bearing in vegetables to the metropolis, but the lines of villas on either side were as silent and lifeless as some city in a dream.

"It has been in some points a singular case," said Holmes, flicking the horse on into a gallop. "I confess that I have been as blind as a mole, but it is better to learn wisdom late than never to learn it at all."

In town the earliest risers were just beginning to look sleepily from their windows as we drove through the streets of the Surrey side.

Passing down the Waterloo Bridge Road, we crossed over the river, and dashing up Wellington Street wheeled sharply to the right and found ourselves in Bow Street. Sherlock Holmes was well known to the force, and the two constables

Barred - *Stopped, Deterred, Provided with one or more bars*
Ledger - *An account book*
Remand – *To send back to custody*
Grating – *Irritating*

at the door saluted him. One of them held the horse's head while the other led us in.

"Who is on duty?" asked Holmes.

"Inspector Bradstreet, sir."

"Ah, Bradstreet, how are you?" A tall, stout official had come down the stone-flagged passage, in a peaked cap and frogged jacket. "I wish to have a quiet word with you, Bradstreet." "Certainly, Mr. Holmes. Step into my room here." It was a small, office-like room, with a huge *ledger* upon the table, and a telephone projecting from the wall. The inspector sat down at his desk.

"What can I do for you, Mr. Holmes?"

"I called about that beggarman, Boone -- the one who was charged with being concerned in the disappearance of Mr. Neville St. Clair, of Lee."

"Yes. He was brought up and *remanded* for further inquiries."

"So I heard. You have him here?"

"In the cells."

"Is he quiet?"

"Oh, he gives no trouble. But he is a dirty scoundrel."

"Dirty?" "Yes, it is all we can do to make him wash his hands, and his face is as black as a tinker's. Well, when once his case has been settled, he will have a regular prison bath; and I think, if you saw him, you would agree with me that he needed it."

"I should like to see him very much."

"Would you? That is easily done. Come this way. You can leave your bag."

"No, I think that I'll take it."

"Very good. Come this way, if you please." He led us down a passage, opened a *barred* door, passed down a winding stair, and brought us to a whitewashed corridor with a line of doors on each side.

"The third on the right is his," said the inspector. "Here it is!" He quietly shot back a panel in the upper part of the door and glanced through.

"He is asleep," said he. "You can see him very well."

Grime - *Make very dirty/filthy*
Tattered - *Torn*
Wheal - *A swelling on the skin*
Sneer - *To smile*
Coarsely – *Roughly*
Repulsive – *Disgusting*
Perpetual – *Continuous*
Horrid – *Unpleasant*

We both put our eyes to the **grating**. The prisoner lay with his face towards us, in a very deep sleep, breathing slowly and heavily. He was a middle-sized man, **coarsely** clad as became his calling, with a coloured shirt protruding through the rent in his **tattered** coat.

He was, as the inspector had said, extremely dirty, but the **grime** which covered his face could not conceal its repulsive ugliness. A broad **wheal** from an old scar ran right across it from eye to chin, and by its contraction had turned up one side of the upper lip, so that three teeth were exposed in a **perpetual** snarl. A shock of very bright red hair grew low over his eyes and forehead.

"He's a beauty, isn't he?" said the inspector.

"He certainly needs a wash," remarked Holmes. "I had an idea that he might, and I took the liberty of bringing the tools with me." He opened the Gladstone bag as he spoke, and took out, to my astonishment, a very large bath-sponge.

"He! he! You are a funny one," chuckled the inspector.

"Now, if you will have the great goodness to open that door very quietly, we will soon make him cut a much more respectable figure."

"Well, I don't know why not," said the inspector. "He doesn't look a credit to the Bow Street cells, does he?" He slipped his key into the lock, and we all very quietly entered the cell. The sleeper half turned, and then settled down once more into a deep slumber. Holmes stooped to the waterjug, moistened his sponge, and then rubbed it twice vigorously across and down the prisoner's face.

"Let me introduce you," he shouted, "to Mr. Neville St. Clair, of Lee, in the county of Kent."

Never in my life have I seen such a sight. The man's face peeled off under the sponge like the bark from a tree. Gone was the coarse brown tint! Gone, too, was the **horrid** scar which had seamed it across, and the twisted lip which had given the repulsive **sneer** to the face!

A twitch brought away the tangled red hair, and there, sitting up in his bed, was a pale, sad-faced, refined-looking man, black-haired and smooth-skinned, rubbing his eyes and staring about him with sleepy bewilderment. Then suddenly

Detain – *Arrest, Withhold, Stop*
Exposure – *Revelation, Display*
Endure – *Tolerate*

realising the exposure, he broke into a scream and threw himself down with his face to the pillow.

"Great heavens!" cried the inspector, "it is, indeed, the missing man. I know him from the photograph." The prisoner turned with the reckless air of a man who abandons himself to his destiny. "Be it so," said he. "And pray what am I charged with?"

"With making away with Mr. Neville St. Oh, come, you can't be charged with that unless they make a case of attempted suicide of it," said the inspector with a grin. "Well, I have been twenty-seven years in the force, but this really takes the cake."

"If I am Mr. Neville St. Clair, then it is obvious that no crime has been committed, and that, therefore, I am illegally *detained*."

"No crime, but a very great error has been committed," said Holmes. "You would have done better to have trusted you wife."

"It was not the wife; it was the children," groaned the prisoner. "God help me, I would not have them ashamed of their father. My God! What an *exposure*! What can I do?"

Sherlock Holmes sat down beside him on the couch and patted him kindly on the shoulder. "If you leave it to a court of law to clear the matter up," said he, "of course, you can hardly avoid publicity. On the other hand, if you convince the police authorities that there is no possible case against you, I do not know that there is any reason that the details should find their way into the papers. Inspector Bradstreet would, I am sure, make notes upon anything which you might tell us and submit it to the proper authorities. The case would then never go into court at all."

"God bless you!" cried the prisoner passionately. "I would have *endured* imprisonment, ay, even execution, rather than have left my miserable secret as a family blot to my children.

"You are the first who have ever heard my story. My father was a school master in Chesterfield, where I received an excellent education. I travelled in my youth, took to the stage, and finally became a reporter on an evening paper in London.

One day my editor wished to have a series of articles upon begging in the metropolis, and I volunteered to supply them.

Ostensibly –
Apparently
Arduous – *Difficult*
Ghastly – *Terrible*
Repartee – *A sharp,*
with tempart

There was the point from which all my adventures started. It was only by trying begging as an amateur that I could get the facts upon which to base my articles.

When an actor I had, of course, learned all the secrets of making up, and had been famous in the greenroom for my skill. I took advantage now of my attainments. I painted my face, and to make myself as pitiable as possible, I made a good scar and fixed one side of my lip in a twist by the aid of a small slip of flesh-coloured plaster.

Then with a red head of hair, and an appropriate dress, I took my station in the business part of the city, **ostensibly** as a match-seller, but really as a beggar. For seven hours, I plied my trade, and when I returned home in the evening, I found to my surprise that I had received no less than 26s. 4d.

"I wrote my articles and thought little more of the matter until, some time later, I backed a bill for a friend and had a writ served upon me for 25 pounds. I was at my wit's end where to get the money, but a sudden idea came to me.

I begged a fortnight's grace from the creditor, asked for a holiday from my employers, and spent the time in begging in the City under my disguise. In ten days, I had the money and had paid the debt.

"Well, you can imagine how hard it was to settle down to **arduous** work at 2 pounds a week when I knew that I could earn as much in a day by smearing my face with a little paint, laying my cap on the ground, and sitting still. It was a long fight between my pride and the money, but the dollars won at last, and I threw up reporting and sat day after day in the corner which I had first chosen, inspiring pity by my **ghastly** face and filling my pockets with coppers.

Only one man knew my secret. He was the keeper of a low den in which I used to lodge in Swandam Lane, where I could every morning emerge as a squalid beggar and in the evenings transform myself into a well-dressed man about town. This fellow, a Lascar, was well paid by me for his rooms, so that I knew that my secret was safe in his possession.

"Well, very soon I found that I was saving considerable sums of money. I do not mean that any beggar in the streets of London could earn 700 pounds a year -- which is less than my average takings -- but I had exceptional advantages in my

Ascend - *Climb*
Scrawl - *Write or draw in an awkward manner*
Horror – *Dismay*
Entreat – *Plead*
Inflict – *Impose*
Prosecute – *Impeach*

power of making up, and also in a facility of *repartee*, which improved by practice and made me quite a recognized character in the City. All day a stream of pennies, varied by silver, poured in upon me, and it was a very bad day in which I failed to take 2 pounds.

"As I grew richer, I grew more ambitious, took a house in the country, and eventually married, without anyone having a suspicion as to my real occupation. My dear wife knew that I had business in the City. She little knew what.

"Last Monday, I had finished for the day and was dressing in my room above the opium den when I looked out of my window and saw, to my horror and astonishment, that my wife was standing in the street, with her eyes fixed full upon me. I gave a cry of surprise, threw up my arms to cover my face, and, rushing to my confidant, the Lascar, *entreated* him to prevent anyone from coming up to me.

I heard her voice downstairs, but I knew that she could not *ascend*. Swiftly, I threw off my clothes, pulled on those of a beggar, and put on my pigments and wig. Even a wife's eyes could not pierce so complete a disguise. But then it occurred to me that there might be a search in the room, and that the clothes might betray me.

I threw open the window, reopening by my violence a small cut which I had inflicted upon myself in the bedroom that morning. Then I seized my coat, which was weighted by the coppers which I had just transferred to it from the leather bag in which I carried my takings. I hurled it out of the window, and it disappeared into the Thames. The other clothes would have followed, but at that moment there was a rush of constables up the stair, and a few minutes after I found, rather, I confess, to my relief, that instead of being identified as Mr. Neville St. Clair, I was arrested as his murderer.

"I do not know that there is anything else for me to explain. I was determined to preserve my disguise as long as possible, and hence, my preference for a dirty face.

Knowing that my wife would be terribly anxious, I slipped off my ring and confided it to the Lascar at a moment when no constable was watching me, together with a hurried *scrawl*, telling her that she had no cause to fear."

Solemn – *Somber*
Oath – *Promise*
Indebted – *Grateful*

"That note only reached her yesterday," said Holmes.

"Good God! What a week she must have spent!"

"The police have watched this Lascar," said Inspector Bradstreet, "and I can quite understand that he might find it difficult to post a letter unobserved. Probably, he handed it to some sailor customer of his, who forgot all about it for some days."

"That was it," said Holmes, nodding approvingly; "I have no doubt of it. But have you never been prosecuted for begging?"

"Many times; but what was a fine to me?"

"It must stop here, however," said Bradstreet. "If the police are to hush this thing up, there must be no more of Hugh Boone."

"I have sworn it by the most *solemn oaths* which a man can take."

"In that case I think that it is probable that no further steps may be taken. But if you are found again, then all must come out. I am sure, Mr. Holmes, that we are very much *indebted* to you for having cleared the matter up. I wish I knew how you reach your results."

"I reached this one," said my friend, "by sitting upon five pillows and consuming an ounce of shag. I think, Watson, that if we drive to Baker Street, we shall just be in time for breakfast."

Food For Thought

Do you think Sherlock Holmes would have been able to solve this mystery if Neville would not have send the letter and the signet ring of his wife?

An Understanding

Q. 1. Where did Watson find Holmes while trying to look for Isa Whitney?

Ans. _____

_____

_____

_____

_____

Q. 2. Who was Neville St. Clair? Why did he dress up as a beggar, whose name was Hugh Boone?

Ans. _____

_____

_____

_____

_____

Q. 3. "Let me introduce you," he shouted, "to Mr. Neville St. Clair, of Lee, in the county of Kent." Who said these words and to whom? Who was the narrator introducing to?

Ans. _____

_____

_____

_____

_____

Q. 4. How did Mr. Neville St. Clair land up in the jail? Narrate briefly.

Ans. _____

_____

_____

_____

_____

The Adventure of the Second Stain

~Arthur Conan Doyle

I had intended "The Adventure of the Abbey Grange" to be the last of those exploits of my friend, Mr. Sherlock Holmes, which I should ever communicate to the public. This resolution of mine was not due to any lack of material, since I have notes of many hundreds of cases to which I have never *alluded*, nor was it caused by any *waning* interest on the part of my readers in the singular personality and unique methods of this remarkable man.

The real reason lay in the reluctance which Mr. Holmes has shown to the continued publication of his experiences. So long as he was in actual professional practice, the records of his successes were of some practical value to him, but since he has definitely retired from London and *betaken* himself to study and bee-farming on the Sussex Downs, *notoriety* has become hateful to him, and he has peremptorily requested that his wishes in this matter should be strictly observed.

It was only upon my representing to him that I had given a promise that "The Adventure of the Second Stain" should be published when the times were ripe, and pointing out to him that it is only appropriate that this long series of episodes should culminate in the most important international case which he has ever been called upon to handle, that I at last succeeded in obtaining his consent that a carefully guarded account of the incident should at last be laid before the public. If in telling the story I seem to be somewhat vague in certain details, the public will readily understand that there is an excellent reason for my *reticence*.

It was, then, in a year, and even in a decade, that shall be nameless, that upon one Tuesday morning in autumn, we found two visitors of European fame within the walls of our humble room in Baker Street. The one, austere, high-nosed, eagle-eyed, and dominant, was none other than the illustrious Lord Bellinger, twice Premier of Britain. The other, dark, clear-cut, and elegant, hardly yet of middle age, and endowed with

Peremptorily - *Dictatorial*
Betaken - *To resort to*
Notoriety - *Ilrepute*
Alluded - *To refer casually*
Waning - *To decrease in strength*
Austere – *Severe*

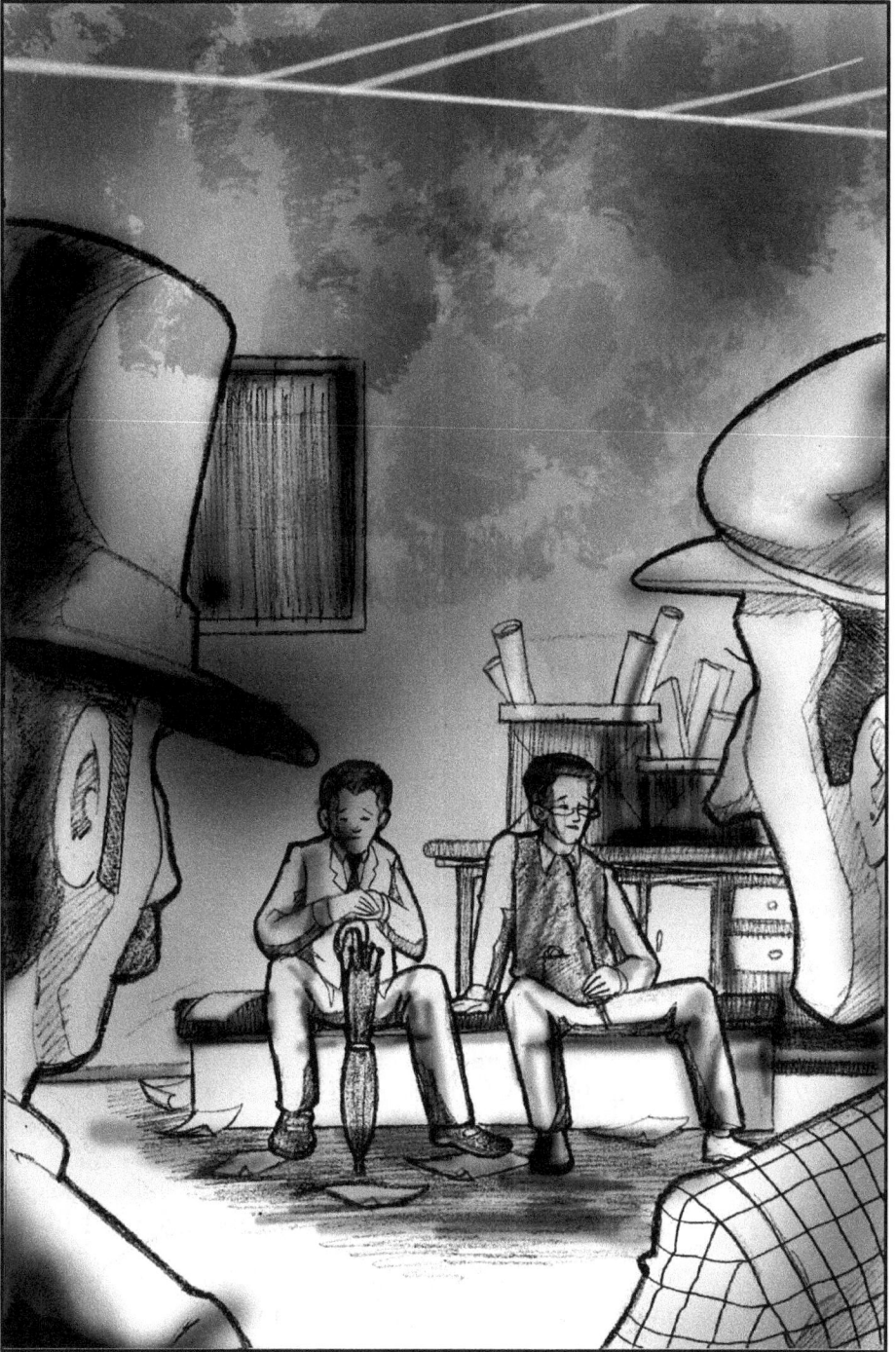

every beauty of body and of mind, was the Right Honourable Trelawney Hope, Secretary for European Affairs, and the most rising statesman in the country.

They sat side by side upon our paper-littered **settee**, and it was easy to see from their worn and anxious faces that it was business of the most pressing importance which had brought them.

The Premier's thin, blue-veined hands were clasped tightly over the ivory head of his umbrella, and his **gaunt**, ascetic face looked gloomily from Holmes to me. The European Secretary pulled nervously at his moustache and **fidgeted** with the seals of his watch-chain.

"When I discovered my loss, Mr. Holmes, which was at eight o'clock this morning, I at once informed the Prime Minister. It was at his suggestion that we have both come to you."

"Have you informed the police?"

"No, sir," said the Prime Minister, with the quick, **decisive** manner for which he was famous. "We have not done so, nor is it possible that we should do so. To inform the police must, in the long run, mean to inform the public. This is what we particularly desire to avoid."

"And why, sir?"

"Because the document in question is of such immense importance that its publication might very easily – I might almost say probably -- lead to European complications of the utmost moment. It is not too much to say that peace or war may hang upon the issue.

Unless its recovery can be attended with the utmost secrecy, then it may as well not be recovered at all, for all that is aimed at by those who have taken it is that its contents should be generally known."

"I understand. Now, Mr. Trelawney Hope, I should be much obliged if you would tell me exactly the circumstances under which this document disappeared."

"That can be done in a very few words, Mr. Holmes. The letter -- for it was a letter from a foreign **potentate** -- was received six days ago. It was of such importance that I have never left it in my safe, but have taken it across each evening to my house in Whitehall Terrace, and kept it in my bedroom in a locked despatch box. It was there last night. Of that I am

Fidgeted - *Make uneasy*
Settee - *A seat for two or more persons*
Gaunt – *Thin*
Decisive – *Important, Conclusive*
Immense – *Huge, Very great*

certain. I actually opened the box, while I was dressing for dinner and saw the document inside. This morning it was gone. The despatch box had stood beside the glass upon my dressing table all night.

I am a light sleeper, and so is my wife. We are both prepared to swear that no one could have entered the room during the night. And yet I repeat that the paper is gone."

"What time did you dine?"

"Half-past seven."

"How long was it before you went to bed?"

"My wife had gone to the theatre. I waited up for her. It was half-past eleven before we went to our room."

"Then for four hours the despatch box had lain unguarded?"

"No one is ever permitted to enter that room save the housemaid in the morning, and my *valet*, or my wife's maid, during the rest of the day. They are both trusty servants who have been with us for some time. Besides, neither of them could possibly have known that there was anything more valuable than the ordinary departmental papers in my despatch box."

"Who did know of the existence of that letter?"

"No one in the house."

"Surely your wife knew?"

"No, sir. I had said nothing to my wife until I missed the paper this morning."

The Premier nodded approvingly.

"I have long known, sir, how high is your sense of public duty," said he. "I am *convinced* that in the case of a secret of this importance, it would rise superior to the most intimate domestic ties.

The European Secretary bowed.

"You do me no more than justice, sir. Until this morning I have never breathed one word to my wife upon this matter."

"Could she have guessed?"

"No, Mr. Holmes, she could not have guessed -- nor could anyone have guessed."

"Have you lost any documents before?"

"No, sir."

Valet - *A male servant*
Convince – *Induce*
Intimate - *Very close*
Pledge – *Vow*

"Who is there in England who did know of the existence of this letter?"

"Each member of the Cabinet was informed of it yesterday, but the **pledge** of secrecy which attends every Cabinet meeting was increased by the solemn warning which was given by the Prime Minister. Good heavens, to think that within a few hours, I should myself have lost it!"

His handsome face was distorted with a **spasm** of **despair**, and his hands tore at his hair. For a moment we caught a **glimpse** of the natural man, **impulsive, ardent**, keenly sensitive. The next the aristocratic mask was replaced, and the gentle voice had returned. "Besides the members of the Cabinet there are two, or possibly three, departmental officials who know of the letter. No one else in England, Mr. Holmes, I assure you."

"But abroad?"

"I believe that no one abroad has seen it save the man who wrote it. I am well convinced that his Ministers — that the usual official channels have not been employed."

Holmes considered for some little time.

"Now, sir, I must ask you more particularly what this document is, and why its disappearance should have such momentous consequences?"

The two statesmen exchanged a quick glance and the Premier's shaggy eyebrows gathered in a frown.

"Mr. Holmes, the envelope is a long, thin one of pale blue colour. There is a seal of red wax stamped with a crouching lion. It is addressed in large, bold handwriting to -- --"

"I fear, sir," said Holmes, "that, interesting and indeed essential as these details are, my inquiries must go more to the root of things. What WAS the letter?"

"That is a State secret of the utmost importance, and I fear that I cannot tell you, nor do I see that it is necessary. If by the aid of the powers which you are said to possess you can find such an envelope as I describe with its enclosure, you will have deserved well of your country, and earned any reward which it lies in our power to **bestow**."

Sherlock Holmes rose with a smile.

"You are two of the most busy men in the country," said he, "and in my own small way, I have also a good many calls upon me. I **regret** exceedingly that I cannot help you in this

Despair – *Misery*
Glimpse – *Sight*
Ardent – *Passionate*
Spasm - *Sudden,*
abnormal pain
Bestow – *Give*
Regret – *Be apologetic*
Resume – *Recommence,*
To begin again

matter, and any continuation of this interview would be a waste of time."

The Premier sprang to his feet with that quick, fierce gleam of his deep-set eyes before which a Cabinet has cowered. "I am not accustomed, sir," he began, but mastered his anger and *resumed* his seat. For a minute or more we all sat in silence. Then the old statesman shrugged his shoulders.

"We must accept your terms, Mr. Holmes. No doubt you are right, and it is unreasonable for us to expect you to act unless we give you our entire confidence."

"I agree with you," said the younger statesman.

"Then I will tell you, relying entirely upon your honour and that of your colleague, Dr. Watson. I may appeal to your patriotism also, for I could not imagine a greater misfortune for the country than that this affair should come out."

"You may safely trust us."

"The letter, then, is from a certain foreign *potentate* who has been *ruffled* by some recent Colonial developments of this country. It has been written hurriedly and upon his own responsibility entirely. Inquiries have shown that his Ministers know nothing of the matter.

At the same time, it is *couched* in so unfortunate a manner, and certain phrases in it are of so provocative a character, that its publication would undoubtedly lead to a most dangerous state of feeling in this country. There would be such a *ferment*, sir, that I do not hesitate to say that within a week of the publication of that letter, this country would be involved in a great war."

Holmes wrote a name upon a slip of paper and handed it to the Premier.

"Exactly. It was he. And it is this letter -- this letter which may well mean the expenditure of a thousand millions and the lives of a hundred thousand men -- which has become lost in this unaccountable fashion."

"Have you informed the sender?"

"Yes, sir, a cipher telegram has been *dispatched*."

"Perhaps, he desires the publication of the letter."

"No, sir, we have strong reason to believe that he already understands that he has acted in an *indiscreet* and hot-headed

Ruffled - *To vex or irritate*
Potentate - *A person of great power*
Ferment – *Uproar*
Dispatch – *Transmit*
Indiscreet – *Careless*

manner. It would be a greater blow to him and to his country than to us if this letter were to come out."

"If this is so, whose interest is it that, the letter should come out? Why should anyone desire to steal it or to publish it?"

"There, Mr. Holmes, you take me into regions of high international politics. But if you consider the European situation you will have no difficulty in perceiving the motive. The whole of Europe is an armed camp.

There is a double league which makes a fair balance of military power. Great Britain holds the scales. If Britain were driven into war with one confederacy, it would assure the supremacy of the other confederacy, whether they joined in the war or not. Do you follow?"

"Very clearly. It is then the interest of the enemies of this potentate to secure and publish this letter, so as to make a **breach** between his country and ours?"

"Yes, sir."

"And to whom would this document be sent if it fell into the hands of an enemy?"

"To any of the great Chancelleries of Europe. It is probably speeding on its way **thither** at the present instant as fast as steam can take it."

Mr. Trelawney Hope dropped his head on his chest and **groaned** aloud. The Premier placed his hand kindly upon his shoulder.

"It is your misfortune, my dear fellow. No one can blame you. There is no precaution which you have neglected. Now, Mr. Holmes, you are in full possession of the facts. What course do you recommend?"

Holmes shook his head mournfully.

"You think, sir, that unless this document is recovered there will be war?"

"I think it is very probable."

"Then, sir, prepare for war."

"That is a hard saying, Mr. Holmes."

"Consider the facts, sir. It is **inconceivable** that it was taken after eleven-thirty at night, since I understand that Mr. Hope and his wife were both in the room from that hour until the loss was found out. It was taken, then, yesterday evening between seven-thirty and eleven-thirty, probably

Thither - *Farther, More remote*
Groaned - *Moaned, a mournful sound*
Breach – *Break*
Inconceivable – *Unthinkable*
Retain – *Keep*

near the earlier hour, since whoever took it evidently knew that it was there and would naturally secure it as early as possible.

Now, sir, if a document of this importance were taken at that hour, where can it be now? No one has any reason to *retain* it. It has been passed rapidly on to those who need it. What chance have we now to overtake or even to trace it? It is beyond our reach."

The Prime Minister rose from the settee.

"What you say is perfectly logical, Mr. Holmes. I feel that the matter is indeed out of our hands."

"Let us *presume*, for argument's sake, that the document was taken by the maid or by the valet -- --"

"They are both old and tried servants."

"I understand you to say that your room is on the second floor, that there is no entrance from without, and that from within no one could go up unobserved. It must, then, be somebody in the house who has taken it.

To whom would the thief take it? To one of several international spies and secret agents, whose names are tolerably familiar to me. There are three who may be said to be the heads of their profession. I will begin my research by going around and finding if each of them is at his post.

If one is missing -- especially, if he has disappeared since last night -- we will have some indication as to where the document has gone."

"Why should he be missing?" asked the European Secretary. "He would take the letter to an Embassy in London, as likely as not."

"I fancy not. These agents work independently, and their relations with the Embassies are often strained."

The Prime Minister nodded his *acquiescence*.

"I believe you are right, Mr. Holmes. He would take so valuable a prize to headquarters with his own hands. I think that your course of action is an excellent one.

Meanwhile, Hope, we cannot neglect all our other duties on account of this one misfortune. Should there be any fresh developments during the, day we shall communicate with you, and you will no doubt let us know the results of your own inquiries."

Gravely - *Seriously*
Presume – *Assume*
Acquiescence – *Agreement*
Illustrious – *Memorable*
Immerse – *Submerge*

The two statesmen bowed and walked *gravely* from the room.

When our *illustrious* visitors had departed, Holmes lit his pipe in silence and sat for some time lost in the deepest thoughts. I had opened the morning paper and was *immersed* in a sensational crime which had occurred in London the night before, when my friend gave an exclamation, sprang to his feet, and laid his pipe down upon the mantelpiece.

"Yes," said he, "there is no better way of approaching it. The situation is desperate, but not hopeless. Even now, if we could be sure which of them has taken it, it is just possible that it has not yet passed out of his hands.

After all, it is a question of money with these fellows, and I have the British treasury behind me. If it's on the market, I'll buy it -- if it means another penny on the income tax. It is conceivable that the fellow might hold it back to see what bids come from this side before he tries his luck on the other.

There are only those three capable of playing so bold a game -- there are *Oberstein, La Rothiere*, and *Eduardo Lucas*. I will see each of them."

I glanced at my morning paper.

"Is that Eduardo Lucas of Godolphin Street?"

"Yes." "You will not see him."

"Why not?"

"He was murdered in his house last night."

My friend has so often astonished me in the course of our adventures that it was with a sense of *exultation* that I realised how completely I had astonished him.

He stared in amazement, and then snatched the paper from my hands. This was the paragraph which I had been engaged in reading when he rose from his chair.

MURDER IN WESTMINSTER

A crime of mysterious character was committed last night at 16 Godolphin Street, one of the old-fashioned and *secluded* rows of the eighteenth century houses which lie between the river and the Abbey, almost in the shadow of the great Tower of the Houses of Parliament.

This small but select mansion has been inhabited for some years by Mr. Eduardo Lucas, well known in society circles, both on account of his charming personality and because he

Ajar - *Slightly open*
Exultation – *Ecstasy*
Secluded – *Private*
Tenor – *Mood*
Transpire – *Become known*

has the well-deserved reputation of being one of the best amateur *tenors* in the country.

Mr. Lucas is an unmarried man, thirty-four years of age, and his establishment consists of Mrs. Pringle, an elderly housekeeper, and of Mitton, his valet. The former retires early and sleeps at the top of the house.

The valet was out for the evening, visiting a friend at Hammersmith. From ten o'clock onward, Mr. Lucas had the house to himself. What occurred during that time has not yet *transpired*, but at a quarter to twelve Police-constable Barrett, passing along Godolphin Street observed that the door of No. 16 was *ajar*.

He knocked, but received no answer. Perceiving a light in the front room, he advanced into the passage and again knocked, but without reply. He then pushed open the door and entered.

The room was in a state of wild disorder, the furniture being all swept to one side, and one chair lying on its back in the centre. Beside this chair, and still grasping one of its legs, lay the unfortunate tenant of the house. He had been stabbed to the heart and must have died instantly.

The knife with which the crime had been committed was a curved Indian dagger, plucked down from a trophy of Oriental arms which *adorned* one of the walls. Robbery does not appear to have been the motive of the crime, for there had been no attempt to remove the valuable contents of the room.

Mr. Eduardo Lucas was so well known and popular that his violent and mysterious fate will arouse painful interest and intense sympathy in a widespread circle of friends.

"Well, Watson, what do you make of this?" asked Holmes, after a long pause.

"It is an amazing coincidence."

"A coincidence! Here is one of the three men whom we had named as possible actors in this drama, and he meets a violent death during the very hours when we know that that drama was being enacted.

The odds are enormous against its being coincidence. No figures could express them. No, my dear Watson, the two events are connected -- must be connected. It is for us to find the connection."

Adorn – *Decorate*
Compress – *Squeeze*
Salver – *Platter*
Modest –
Unassuming

"But now the official police must know all."

"Not at all. They know all they see at Godolphin Street. They know -- and shall know -- nothing of Whitehall Terrace. Only WE know of both events, and can trace the relation between them. There is one obvious point which would, in any case, have turned my suspicions against Lucas.

Godolphin Street, Westminster, is only a few minutes' walk from Whitehall Terrace. The other secret agents whom I have named live in the extreme West End. It was easier, therefore, for Lucas than for the others to establish a connection or receive a message from the European Secretary's household -- a small thing, and yet where events are compressed into a few hours, it may prove essential. Halloa! what have we here?"

Mrs. Hudson had appeared with a lady's card upon her *salver*. Holmes glanced at it, raised his eyebrows, and handed it over to me.

"Ask Lady Hilda Trelawney Hope if she will be kind enough to step up," said he.

A moment later our *modest* apartment, already so distinguished that morning, was further honoured by the entrance of the most lovely woman in London.

I had often heard of the beauty of the youngest daughter of the Duke of Belminster, but no description of it, and no *contemplation* of colourless photographs, had prepared me for the *subtle*, delicate charm, and the beautiful colouring of that *exquisite* head. And yet as we saw it that autumn morning, it was not its beauty which would be the first thing to impress the observer.

The cheek was lovely, but it was paled with emotion, the eyes were bright but it was the brightness of fever, the sensitive mouth was tight and drawn in an effort after self-command. Terror -- not beauty -- was what sprang first to the eye as our fair visitor stood framed for an instant in the open door.

"Has my husband been here, Mr. Holmes?"

"Yes, madam, he has been here."

"Mr. Holmes. I *implore* you not to tell him that I came here." Holmes bowed coldly, and motioned the lady to a chair.

"Your ladyship places me in a very delicate position. I beg that you will sit down and tell me what you desire, but I fear that I cannot make any unconditional promise."

Deplorable - *Shockingly bad in quality*
Clasped - *Grasped tightly with one's hand*
Subtle – *Slight*
Exquisite – *Beautiful*
Implore – *Beg*
Induce – *Persuade*

She swept across the room and seated herself with her back to the window. It was a queenly presence -- tall, graceful, and intensely womanly. "Mr. Holmes," she said -- and her white-gloved hands *clasped* and unclasped as she spoke --" I will speak frankly to you in the hopes that it may *induce* you to speak frankly in return.

There is complete confidence between my husband and me on all matters save one. That one is politics. On this his lips are sealed. He tells me nothing. Now, I am aware that there was a most *deplorable* occurrence in our house last night. I know that a paper has disappeared. But because the matter is political, my husband refuses to take me into his complete confidence.

Now it is essential -- essential, I say -- that I should thoroughly understand it. You are the only other person, save only these politicians, who knows the facts. I beg you then, Mr. Holmes, to tell me exactly what has happened and what it will lead to. Tell me all, Mr. Holmes.

Let no regard for your client's interests keep you silent, for I assure you that his interests, if he would only see it, would be best served by taking me into his complete confidence. What was this paper which was stolen?"

"Madam, what you ask me is really impossible."

She groaned and sank her face in her hands.

"You must see that this is so, madam. If your husband thinks fit to keep you in the dark over this matter, is it for me, who has only learned the facts under the *pledge* of professional secrecy, to tell what he has withheld? It is not fair to ask it. It is him whom you must ask."

"I have asked him. I come to you as a last resource. But without your telling me anything definite, Mr. Holmes, you may do a great service if you would *enlighten* me on one point."

"What is it, madam?"

"Is my husband's political career likely to suffer through this incident?"

"Well, madam, unless it is set right, it may certainly have a very unfortunate effect."

"Ah!" She drew in her breath sharply as one whose doubts are resolved.

Pledge – *Vow*
Enlighten – *Inform, Edify*
Dwindling – *Declining*
Tenacity – *Stubbornness*

"One more question, Mr. Holmes. From an expression which my husband dropped in the first shock of this disaster, I understood that terrible public consequences might arise from the loss of this document."

"If he said so, I certainly cannot deny it."

"Of what nature are they?"

"Nay, madam, there again you ask me more than I can possibly answer."

"Then I will take up no more of your time. I cannot blame you, Mr. Holmes, for having refused to speak more freely, and you on your side will not, I am sure, think the worse of me because I desire, even against his will, to share my husband's anxieties. Once more I beg that you will say nothing of my visit."

She looked back at us from the door, and I had a last impression of that beautiful haunted face, the startled eyes, and the drawn mouth. Then she was gone.

"Now, Watson, the fair sex is your department," said Holmes, with a smile, when the *dwindling* frou-frou of skirts had ended in the slam of the front door. "What was the fair lady's game? What did she really want?"

"Surely her own statement is clear and her anxiety very natural."

"Hum! Think of her appearance, Watson -- her manner, her suppressed excitement, her restlessness, her *tenacity* in asking questions. Remember that she comes of a caste who do not lightly show emotion."

"She was certainly much moved."

"Remember also the curious earnestness with which she assured us that it was best for her husband that she should know all. What did she mean by that? And you must have observed, Watson, how she *manoeuvred* to have the light at her back. She did not wish us to read her expression."

"Yes, she chose the one chair in the room."

"And yet the motives of women are so *inscrutable*. You remember the woman at Margate whom I suspected for the same reason. No powder on her nose -- that proved to be the correct solution. How can you build on such a quicksand? Their most *trivial* action may mean volumes, or their most extraordinary conduct may depend upon a hairpin or a curling tongs. Good morning, Watson."

Indefatigable - *Untiring*
Inscrutable - *Mysterious*
Manoeuvred - *Contrived*
Taciturn - *Saying little*
Reveries - *Daydreams*
Inkling - *A hint*
Inquest – *Investigation*
Tamper – *Interfere*

"You are off?"

"Yes, I will while away the morning at Godolphin Street with our friends of the regular establishment. With Eduardo Lucas lies the solution of our problem, though I must admit that I have not an *inkling* as to what form it may take. It is a capital mistake to theorise in advance of the facts. Do stay on guard, my good Watson, and receive any fresh visitors. I'll join you at lunch if I am able."

All that day and the next and the next Holmes was in a mood which his friends would call *taciturn*, and others morose. He ran out and ran in, smoked incessantly, played snatches on his violin, sank into *reveries*, devoured sandwiches at irregular hours, and hardly answered the casual questions which I put to him.

It was evident to me that things were not going well with him or his quest. He would say nothing of the case, and it was from the papers that I learned the particulars of the inquest, and the arrest with the subsequent release of John Mitton, the valet of the deceased. The coroner's jury brought in the obvious Wilful Murder, but the parties remained as unknown as ever. No motive was suggested.

The room was full of articles of value, but none had been taken. The dead man's papers had not been tampered with. They were carefully examined, and showed that he was a keen student of international politics, an *indefatigable* gossip, a remarkable linguist, and an untiring letter writer. He had been on intimate terms with the leading politicians of several countries. But nothing sensational was discovered among the documents which filled his drawers.

As to his relations with women, they appeared to have been *promiscuous* but *superficial*. He had many acquaintances among them, but few friends, and no one whom he loved. His habits were regular, his conduct *inoffensive*. His death was an absolute mystery and likely to remain so.

As to the arrest of John Mitton, the valet, it was a council of despair as an alternative to absolute inaction. But no case could be sustained against him. He had visited friends in Hammersmith that night. The *alibi* was complete. It is true that he started home at an hour which should have brought him to Westminster before the time when the crime was discovered, but his own explanation that he had walked part of

Corroborate - *Confirm or give to support*

Promiscuous *- Having many sexual relationships*

Superficial *– Trivial Shallow*

Inoffensive *– Innocuous*

Despair *– Misery*

Alibi *– Explanation*

the way seemed probable enough in view of the fineness of the night. He had actually arrived at twelve o'clock, and appeared to be overwhelmed by the unexpected tragedy. He had always been on good terms with his master.

Several of the dead man's possessions -- notably a small case of razors -- had been found in the valet's boxes, but he explained that they had been presents from the deceased, and the housekeeper was able to *corroborate* the story. Mitton had been in Lucas's employment for three years.

It was noticeable that Lucas did not take Mitton on the Continent with him. Sometimes he visited Paris for three months on end, but Mitton was left in charge of the Godolphin Street house. As to the housekeeper, she had heard nothing on the night of the crime. If her master had a visitor, he had himself admitted him.

So for three mornings the mystery remained, so far as I could follow it in the papers. If Holmes knew more, he kept his own counsel, but, as he told me that Inspector Lestrade had taken him into his confidence in the case, I knew that he was in close touch with every development. Upon the fourth day, there appeared a long telegram from Paris which seemed to solve the whole question.

A discovery has just been made by the Parisian police a [said the *Daily Telegraph*] which raises the veil which hung round the tragic fate of Mr. Eduardo Lucas, who met his death by violence last Monday night at Godolphin Street, Westminster.

Our readers will remember that the deceased gentleman was found stabbed in his room, and that some suspicion attached to his valet, but that the case broke down on an alibi. Yesterday a lady, who has been known as Mme. Henri Fournaye, occupying a small villa in the Rue Austerlitz, was reported to the authorities by her servants as being *insane*. An examination showed she had indeed developed mania of a dangerous and permanent form. On inquiry, the police have discovered that Mme.

Henri Fournaye only returned from a journey to London on Tuesday last, and there is evidence to connect her with the crime at Westminster. A comparison of photographs has proved conclusively that M. Henri Fournaye and Eduardo Lucas were really one and the same person, and that the

Gestures - *Body movements*
Frenzy - *Fury, rage, or excitement*
Conjectured - *Form an opinion*
Insane - *Mad*
Mania – *Obsession*
Catastrophe – *Disaster*

deceased had for some reason lived a double life in London and Paris. Mme. Fournaye, who is of Creole origin, is of an extremely excitable nature, and has suffered in the past from attacks of jealousy which have amounted to *frenzy*.

It is *conjectured* that it was in one of these that she committed the terrible crime which has caused such a sensation in London. Her movements upon Monday night have not yet been traced, but it is undoubted that a woman answering to her description attracted much attention at Charing Cross Station on Tuesday morning by the wildness of her appearance and the violence of her *gestures*.

It is probable, therefore, that the crime was either committed when insane, or that its immediate effect was to drive the unhappy woman out of her mind. At present, she is unable to give any coherent account of the past, and the doctors hold out no hopes of the reestablishment of her reason. There is evidence that a woman, who might have been Mme. Fournaye, was seen for some hours upon Monday night watching the house in Godolphin Street.

"What do you think of that, Holmes?" I had read the account aloud to him, while he finished his breakfast.

"My dear Watson," said he, as he rose from the table and paced up and down the room, "You are most long-suffering, but if I have told you nothing in the last three days, it is because there is nothing to tell. Even now this report from Paris does not help us much."

"Surely it is final as regards the man's death."

"The man's death is a mere incident -- a trivial episode -- in comparison with our real task, which is to trace this document and save a European catastrophe. Only one important thing has happened in the last three days, and that is that nothing has happened. I get reports almost hourly from the government, and it is certain that nowhere in Europe is there any sign of trouble.

Now, if this letter were loose -- no, it can't be loose -- but if it isn't loose, where can it be? Who has it? Why is it held back? That's the question that beats in my brain like a hammer. Was it, indeed, a coincidence that Lucas should meet his death on the night when the letter disappeared? Did the letter ever reach him? If so, why is it not among his papers? Did this mad wife of his carry it off with her? If so, is it in her house in Paris?

Effeminacy - *Having femine qualities*
Suspicion – *Doubt*
Colossal – *Huge*
Magnificent – *Superb*
Sumptuous – *Luxurious*
Reproach – *Criticism*

How could I search for it without the French police having their *suspicions* aroused? It is a case, my dear Watson, where the law is as dangerous to us as the criminals are. Every man's hand is against us, and yet the interests at stake are *colossal*.

Should I bring it to a successful conclusion, it will certainly represent the crowning glory of my career. Ah, here is my latest from the front!" He glanced hurriedly at the note which had been handed in. "Halloa! Lestrade seems to have observed something of interest. Put on your hat, Watson, and we will stroll down together to Westminster."

It was my first visit to the scene of the crime -- a high, dingy, narrow-chested house, prim, formal, and solid, like the century which gave it birth.

Lestrade's bulldog features gazed out at us from the front window, and he greeted us warmly when a big constable had opened the door and let us in. The room into which we were shown was that in which the crime had been committed, but no trace of it now remained save an ugly, irregular stain upon the carpet.

This carpet was a small square drugget in the centre of the room, surrounded by a broad expanse of beautiful, old-fashioned wood flooring in square blocks, highly polished. Over the fireplace was a *magnificent* trophy of weapons, one of which had been used on that tragic night.

In the window was a *sumptuous* writing desk, and every detail of the apartment, the pictures, the rugs, and the hangings, all pointed to a taste which was luxurious to the verge of *effeminacy*.

"Seen the Paris news?" asked Lestrade.

Holmes nodded.

"Our French friends seem to have touched the spot this time. No doubt it's just as they say. She knocked at the door -- surprise visit, I guess, for he kept his life in watertight compartments -- he let her in, couldn't keep her in the street. She told him how she had traced him, *reproached* him.

One thing led to another, and then with that dagger so handy the end soon came. It wasn't all done in an instant, though, for these chairs were all swept over yonder, and he had one in his hand as if he had tried to hold her off with it. We've got it all clear as if we had seen it."

Holmes raised his eyebrows.

Freakish - *Abnormal*
Anxiety –
Nervousness
Correspond –
Communicate

"And yet you have sent for me?"

"Ah, yes, that's another matter -- a mere trifle, but the sort of thing you take an interest in -- queer, you know, and what you might call *freakish*. It has nothing to do with the main fact -- can't have, on the face of it."

"What is it, then?"

"Well, you know, after a crime of this sort, we are very careful to keep things in their position. Nothing has been moved. Officer in charge here day and night. This morning, as the man was buried and the investigation over -- so far as this room is concerned -- we thought we could tidy up a bit. This carpet. You see, it is not fastened down, only just laid there. We had occasion to raise it. We found -- --"

"Yes? You found -- --"

Holmes's face grew tense with *anxiety*.

"Well, I'm sure you would never guess in a hundred years what we did find. You see that stain on the carpet? Well, a great deal must have soaked through, must it not?"

"Undoubtedly it must."

"Well, you will be surprised to hear that there is no stain on the white woodwork to correspond."

"No stain! But there must -- --"

"Yes, so you would say. But the fact remains that there isn't."

He took the corner of the carpet in his hand and, turning it over, he showed that it was indeed as he said.

"But the under side is as stained as the upper. It must have left a mark."

Lestrade chuckled with delight at having puzzled the famous expert.

"Now, I'll show you the explanation. There is a second stain, but it does not correspond with the other. See for yourself." As he spoke, he turned over another portion of the carpet, and there, sure enough, was a great crimson spill upon the square white facing of the old-fashioned floor. "What do you make of that, Mr. Holmes?"

"Why, it is simple enough. The two stains did correspond, but the carpet has been turned around. As it was square and unfastened it was easily done."

"The official police don't need you, Mr. Holmes, to tell them that the carpet must have been turned around. That's clear enough, for the stains lie above each other -- if you lay it over

Drugget - *A rug made of coarse fabric*
Paroxysm – *Convulsion*
Languidly – *Unenergetically*
Inexcusable – *Unforgivable*

this way. But what I want to know is, who shifted the carpet, and why?"

I could see from Holmes's rigid face that he was vibrating with inward excitement.

"Look here, Lestrade," said he, "has that constable in the passage been in charge of the place all the time?"

"Yes, he has."

"Well, take my advice. Examine him carefully. Don't do it before us. Well wait here. You take him into the back room. You'll be more likely to get a confession out of him alone. Ask him how he dared to admit people and leave them alone in this room.

Don't ask him if he has done it. Take it for granted. Tell him you know someone has been here. Press him. Tell him that a full confession is his only chance of forgiveness. Do exactly what I tell you!"

"By George, if he knows I'll have it out of him!" cried Lestrade. He darted into the hall, and a few moments later, his bullying voice sounded from the back room.

"Now, Watson, now!" cried Holmes with frenzied eagerness. All the demoniacal force of the man masked behind that listless manner burst out in a *paroxysm* of energy.

He tore the *drugget* from the floor, and in an instant was down on his hands and knees clawing at each of the squares of wood beneath it. One turned sideways as he dug his nails into the edge of it. It hinged back like the lid of a box. A small black cavity opened beneath it. Holmes plunged his eager hand into it and drew it out with a bitter snarl of anger and disappointment. It was empty.

"Quick, Watson, quick! Get it back again!" The wooden lid was replaced, and the drugget had only just been drawn straight when Lestrade's voice was heard in the passage. He found Holmes leaning *languidly* against the mantelpiece, resigned and patient, endeavouring to conceal his irrepressible yawns.

"Sorry to keep you waiting, Mr. Holmes . I can see that you are bored to death with the whole affair. Well, he has confessed, all right. Come in here, MacPherson. Let these gentlemen hear of your most *inexcusable* conduct."

The big constable, very hot and *penitent, sidled* into the room.

Sidled - *Walk in a timid manner*
Penitent – *Repentant*
Genteel – *Refined*

"I meant no harm, sir, I'm sure. The young woman came to the door last evening -- mistook the house, she did. And then we got talking. It's lonesome, when you're on duty here all day."

"Well, what happened then?"

"She wanted to see where the crime was done -- had read about it in the papers, she said. She was a very respectable, well-spoken young woman, sir, and I saw no harm in letting her have a peep. When she saw that mark on the carpet, down she dropped on the floor, and lay as if she were dead.

I ran to the back and got some water, but I could not bring her to. Then I went around the corner to the Ivy Plant for some brandy, and by the time I had brought it back the young woman had recovered and was off -- ashamed of herself, I daresay, and dared not face me."

"How about moving that drugget?"

"Well, sir, it was a bit rumpled, certainly, when I came back. You see, she fell on it and it lies on a polished floor with nothing to keep it in place. I straightened it out afterwards."

"It's a lesson to you that you can't deceive me, Constable MacPherson," said Lestrade, with dignity. "No doubt you thought that your breach of duty could never be discovered, and yet a mere glance at that drugget was enough to convince me that someone had been admitted to the room.

It's lucky for you, my man, that nothing is missing, or you would find yourself in Queer Street. I'm sorry to have called you down over such a petty business, Mr. Holmes, but I thought the point of the second stain not corresponding with the first would interest you."

"Certainly, it was most interesting. Has this woman only been here once, constable?"

"Yes, sir, only once."

"Who was she?"

"Don't know the name, sir. Was answering an advertisement about typewriting and came to the wrong number -- very pleasant, *genteel* young woman, sir."

"Tall? Handsome?"

"Yes, sir, she was a well-grown young woman. I suppose you might say she was handsome. Perhaps some would say she was very handsome. 'Oh, officer, do let me have a peep!' says she. She had pretty, *coaxing* ways, as you might say, and I thought there was no harm in letting her just put her head through the door."

Coax – *Persuade*
Intently - *Attentively*
Indignation – *Resentment*
Ungenerous – *Stingy*
Intrude – *Encroach*

"How was she dressed?"

"Quiet, sir -- a long mantle down to her feet."

"What time was it?"

"It was just growing dusk at the time. They were lighting the lamps as I came back with the brandy." "Very good," said Holmes. "Come, Watson, I think that we have more important work elsewhere." As we left the house, Lestrade remained in the front room, while the *repentant* constable opened the door to let us out. Holmes turned on the step and held up something in his hand. The constable stared *intently*.

"Good Lord, sir!" he cried, with amazement on his face. Holmes put his finger on his lips, replaced his hand in his breast pocket, and burst out laughing as we turned down the street. "Excellent!" said he. "Come, friend Watson, the curtain rings up for the last act.

You will be relieved to hear that there will be no war, that the Right Honourable Trelawney Hope will suffer no setback in his brilliant career, that the indiscreet Sovereign will receive no punishment for his indiscretion, that the Prime Minister will have no European complication to deal with, and that with a little tact and management upon our part nobody will be a penny the worse for what might have been a very ugly incident."

My mind filled with admiration for this extraordinary man.

"You have solved it!" I cried.

"Hardly that, Watson. There are some points which are as dark as ever. But we have so much that it will be our own fault if we cannot get the rest. We will go straight to Whitehall Terrace and bring the matter to a head."

When we arrived at the residence of the European Secretary, it was for Lady Hilda Trelawney Hope that Sherlock Holmes inquired. We were shown into the morning room.

"Mr. Holmes!" said the lady, and her face was pink with her *indignation*. "This is surely most unfair and ungenerous upon your part. I desired, as I have explained, to keep my visit to you a secret, lest my husband should think that I was *intruding* into his affairs. And yet you compromise me by coming here and so showing that there are business relations between us."

Rallied - *Bring together*
Totter – *Falter*
Darted - *Move suddenly or rapidly*
Browbeat – *Bully*

"Unfortunately, madam, I had no possible alternative. I have been commissioned to recover this immensely important paper. I must therefore ask you, madam, to be kind enough to place it in my hands."

The lady sprang to her feet, with the colour all *dashed* in an instant from her beautiful face. Her eyes glazed -- she *tottered* -- I thought that she would faint. Then with a grand effort, she rallied from the shock, and a supreme astonishment and indignation chased every other expression from her features.

"You -- you insult me, Mr. Holmes."

"Come, come, madam, it is useless. Give up the letter."

She darted to the bell.

"The butler shall show you out."

"Do not ring, Lady Hilda. If you do, then all my earnest efforts to avoid a scandal will be frustrated. Give up the letter and all will be set right. If you will work with me, I can arrange everything. If you work against me, I must expose you."

She stood grandly defiant, a queenly figure, her eyes fixed upon his as if she would read his very soul. Her hand was on the bell, but she had *forborne* to ring it.

"You are trying to frighten me. It is not a very manly thing, Mr. Holmes, to come here and browbeat a woman. You say that you know something. What is it that you know?"

"Pray sit down, madam. You will hurt yourself there if you fall. I will not speak until you sit down. Thank you."

"I give you five minutes, Mr. Holmes."

"One is enough, Lady Hilda. I know of your visit to Eduardo Lucas, of your giving him this document, of your ingenious return to the room last night, and of the manner in which you took the letter from the hiding place under the carpet."

She stared at him with an ashen face and gulped twice before she could speak.

"You are mad, Mr. Holmes -- you are mad!" she cried, at last.

He drew a small piece of cardboard from his pocket. It was the face of a woman cut out of a portrait. "I have carried this because I thought it might be useful," said he. "The policeman has recognised it."

She gave a gasp, and her head dropped back in the chair.

"Come, Lady Hilda. You have the letter. The matter may still be adjusted. I have no desire to bring trouble to you. My duty ends when I have returned the lost letter to your husband. Take my advice and be frank with me. It is your only chance."

Her courage was admirable. Even now she would not own defeat.

Absurd – *Ridiculous*
Supplication - *To ask humbly*

the lady.

r senses eve

Where is th

cross to a w

velope.

Ir. Holmes.

fore my hus

urn my lette

escribed in r

who had to

could com

thrust the document into some hiding place there, and covered it over.

"What happened after that is like some fearful dream. I have a vision of a dark, *frantic* face, of a woman's voice, which screamed in French, 'My waiting is not in vain. At last, at last I have found you with her!' There was a savage struggle. I saw him with a chair in his hand, a knife gleamed in hers. I rushed from the horrible scene, ran from the house, and only next morning in the paper did I learn the dreadful result. That night I was happy, for I had my letter, and I had not seen yet what the future would bring.

"It was the next morning that I realised that I had only exchanged one trouble for another. My husband's **anguish** at the loss of his paper went to my heart. I could hardly prevent myself from there and then kneeling down at his feet and telling him what I had done. But that again would mean a confession of the past. I came to you that morning in order to understand the full enormity of my *offence*.

From the instant that I grasped it my whole mind was turned to the one thought of getting back my husband's paper. It must still be where Lucas had placed it, for it was concealed before this dreadful woman entered the room. If it had not been for her coming, I should not have known where his hiding place was. How was I to get into the room? For two days, I watched the place, but the door was never left open.

Last night, I made a last attempt. What I did and how I succeeded, you have already learned. I brought the paper back with me, and thought of destroying it, since I could see no way of returning it without confessing my guilt to my husband. Heavens, I hear his step upon the stair!"

The European Secretary burst excitedly into the room. "Any news, Mr. Holmes, any news?" he cried.

"I have some hopes."

"Ah, thank heaven!" His face became *radiant*. "The Prime Minister is lunching with me. May he share your hopes? He has nerves of steel, and yet I know that he has hardly slept since this terrible event. Jacobs, will you ask the Prime Minister to come up? As to you, dear, I fear that this is a matter of politics. We will join you in a few minutes in the dining room."

Twitchings - *To give short, sudden jerkings*
Conceivably - *Imaginably*
Subdued – *Passive*
Radiant – *Happy*
Apprehend – *To understand*
Assurance – *Pledge*
Presume – *Assume*

The Prime Minister's manner was *subdued,* but I could see by the gleam of his eyes and the *twitchings* of his bony hands that he shared the excitement of his young colleague.

"I understand that you have something to report, Mr. Holmes?"

"Purely negative as yet," my friend answered. "I have inquired at every point where it might be, and I am sure that there is no danger to be *apprehended.*"

"But that is not enough, Mr. Holmes. We cannot live forever on such a volcano. We must have something definite."

"I am in hopes of getting it. That is why I am here. The more I think of the matter, the more convinced I am that the letter has never left this house."

"Mr. Holmes!"

"If it had, it would certainly have been public by now."

"But why should anyone take it in order to keep it in his house?"

"I am not convinced that anyone did take it."

"Then how could it leave the despatch box?"

"I am not convinced that it ever did leave the despatch box."

"Mr. Holmes, this joking is very ill-timed. You have my assurance that it left the box."

"Have you examined the box since Tuesday morning?"

"No. It was not necessary."

"You may conceivably have overlooked it."

"Impossible, I say."

"But I am not convinced of it. I have known such things to happen. I presume there are other papers there. Well, it may have got mixed with them."

"It was on the top."

"Someone may have shaken the box and displaced it."

"No, no, I had everything out."

"Surely it is easily, decided, Hope," said the Premier. "Let us have the despatch box brought in."

The Secretary rang the bell.

"Jacobs, bring down my despatch-box. This is a *farcical* waste of time, but still, if nothing else will satisfy you, it shall be done. Thank you, Jacobs, put it here. I have always had the key on my watch chain. Here are the papers, you see. Letter from

Wizard - *A magician*
Sorcerer - *A person who practises witchcraft*
Farcical – *Ridiculous*
Intact – *Whole*
Inconceivable – *Unthinkable*

Lord Merrow, report from Sir Charles Hardy, memorandum from Belgrade, note on the Russo-German grain taxes, letter from Madrid, note from Lord Flowers -- -- Good heavens! What is this? Lord Bellinger! Lord Bellinger!"

The Premier snatched the blue envelope from his hand.

"Yes, it is it -- and the letter is intact. Hope, I congratulate you."

"Thank you! Thank you! What a weight from my heart. But this is *inconceivable* -- impossible. Mr. Holmes, you are a *wizard*, a *sorcerer*! How did you know it was there?"

"Because I knew it was nowhere else."

"I cannot believe my eyes!" He ran wildly to the door. "Where is my wife? I must tell her that all is well. Hilda! Hilda!" We heard his voice on the stairs.

The Premier looked at Holmes with twinkling eyes.

"Come, sir," said he. "There is more in this than meets the eye. How came the letter back in the box?"

Holmes turned away smiling from the keen scrutiny of those wonderful eyes.

"We also have our diplomatic secrets," said he and, picking up his hat, he turned to the door.

Food For Thought

What would have been the conclusion of this story if Sherlock Holmes would have revealed Lady Hilda's secret to the Prime Minister or her husband? Why didn't he do so?

An Understanding

Q. 1. Why did Lord Bellinger, twice Premier of Britain and Trelawney Hope, Secretary for European Affairs visit Holmes?

Ans. _____

_____

_____

_____

_____

Q. 2. "That is a state secret of utmost importance, I fear that I cannot tell you, nor do I see that it is necessary." Who spoke these words to whom and why?

Ans. _____

_____

_____

_____

_____

Q. 3. Do you think that *The Adventure of the Second Stain* is an apt heading for this story? If Yes, then why? And if 'No', then suggest another suitable heading for this story. Also give reason as to why you changed the heading?

Ans. _____

_____

_____

_____

_____

Q. 4. "Good Lord, sir!" Who said these words to whom and why? Why did Holmes put his finger on the lips of the speaker who said the above words?

Ans. _____

_____

_____

_____

_____

The Adventure of the Norwood Builder

~ Arthur Conan Doyle

"**F**rom the point of view of the criminal expert," said Mr. Sherlock Holmes, "London has become a singularly uninteresting city since the death of the late lamented Professor Moriarty."

"I can hardly think that you would find many decent citizens to agree with you," I answered.

"Well, well, I must not be selfish," said he, with a smile, as be pushed back his chair from the breakfast table. "The community is certainly the gainer, and no one the loser, save the poor out-of-work specialist, whose occupation has gone. With that man in the field, one's morning paper presented *infinite* possibilities. Often it was only the smallest trace, Watson, the faintest indication, and yet it was enough to tell me that the great *malignant* brain was there, as the gentlest tremors of the edges of the web remind one of the *foul* spider which *lurks* in the centre. Petty thefts, wanton assaults, purposeless *outrage* to the man who held the clue that all could be worked into one connected whole. To the scientific student of the higher criminal world, no capital in Europe offered the advantages which London then possessed. But now -- --" He shrugged his shoulders in humorous *deprecation* of the state of things which he had himself done so much to produce.

At the time of which I speak, Holmes had been back for some months, and I at his request had sold my practice and returned to share the old quarters in Baker Street. A young doctor, named Verner, had purchased my small Kensington practice, and given with astonishingly little *demur* the highest price that I ventured to ask -- an incident which only explained itself some years later, when I found that Verner was a distant relation of Holmes, and that it was my friend who had really found the money.

Our months of partnership had not been so uneventful as he had stated, for I find, on looking over my notes, that this period includes the case of the papers of ex-President Murillo, and also the shocking affair of the Dutch steamship

Foul - *Disgusting smell*
Lurks - *Remain hidden*
Infinite – *Never ending*
Malignant – *Evil*
Deprecation - *Denounee, Condemn*
Demur - *Raise doubts or objection*

Friesland, which so nearly cost us both our lives. His cold and proud nature was always *averse*, however, from anything in the shape of public applause, and he bound me in the most *stringent* terms to say no further word of himself, his methods, or his successes -- a prohibition which, as I have explained, has only now been removed.

Mr. Sherlock Holmes was leaning back in his chair after his *whimsical* protest, and was unfolding his morning paper in a leisurely fashion, when our attention was arrested by a tremendous ring at the bell, followed immediately by a hollow drumming sound, as if someone were beating on the outer door with his fist. As it opened, there came a *tumultuous* rush into the hall, rapid feet clattered up the stairs, and an instant later a wild-eyed and frantic young man, pale, *disheveled*, and *palpitating*, burst into the room. He looked from one to the other of us, and under our gaze of inquiry, he became conscious that some apology was needed for this unceremonious entry.

"I'm sorry, Mr. Holmes," he cried. "You mustn't blame me. I am nearly mad. Mr. Holmes, I am the unhappy John Hector McFarlane."

He made the announcement as if the name alone would explain both his visit and its manner, but I could see, by my companion's *unresponsive* face, that it meant no more to him than to me.

"Have a cigarette, Mr. McFarlane," said he, pushing his case across. "I am sure that, with your symptoms, my friend, Dr. Watson here would prescribe a sedative. The weather has been so very warm these last few days. Now, if you feel a little more composed, I should be glad if you would sit down in that chair, and tell us very slowly and quietly who you are, and what it is that you want. You mentioned your name, as if I should recognise it, but I assure you that, beyond the obvious facts that you are a bachelor, a solicitor, a Freemason, and an asthmatic, I know nothing whatever about you."

Familiar as I was with my friend's methods, it was not difficult for me to follow his deductions, and to observe the untidiness of attire, the sheaf of legal papers, the watch-charm, and the breathing which had prompted them. Our client, however, stared in amazement.

"Yes, I am all that, Mr. Holmes; and, in addition, I am the most unfortunate man at this moment in London. For heaven's

Averse – *Reluctant*
Stringent - *Strict*
Whimsical – *Fanciful*
Tumultuous – *Turbulent*
Dishevelled – *Messy*
Unresponsive – *Unfeeling*
Attire – *Clothing*

sake, don't *abandon* me, Mr. Holmes! If they come to arrest me before I have finished my story, make them give me time, so that I may tell you the whole truth. I could go to jail happy if I knew that you were working for me outside."

"Arrest you!" said Holmes. "This is really most grati -- most interesting. On what charge do you expect to be arrested?"

"Upon the charge of murdering Mr. Jonas Oldacre, of Lower Norwood."

My companion's expressive face showed a sympathy which was not, I am afraid, entirely unmixed with satisfaction.

"Dear me," said he, "it was only this moment at breakfast that I was saying to my friend, Dr. Watson, that sensational cases had disappeared out of our papers."

Our visitor stretched forward a *quivering* hand and picked up the Daily Telegraph, which still lay upon Holmes's knee.

"If you had looked at it, sir, you would have seen at a glance what the *errand* is on which I have come to you this morning. I feel as if my name and my misfortune must be in every man's mouth." He turned it over to expose the central page. "Here it is, and with your permission, I will read it to you. Listen to this, Mr. Holmes. The headlines are: 'Mysterious Affair at Lower Norwood. Disappearance of a Well-known Builder. Suspicion of Murder and Arson. A Clue to the Criminal.' That is the clue which they are already following, Mr. Holmes, and I know that it leads *infallibly* to me. I have been followed from London Bridge Station, and I am sure that they are only waiting for the *warrant* to arrest me. It will break my mother's heart -- it will break her heart!" He *wrung* his hands in an agony of *apprehension*, and swayed backward and forward in his chair.

I looked with interest upon this man, who was accused of being the *perpetrator* of a crime of violence. He was flaxen-haired and handsome, in a washed-out negative fashion, with frightened blue eyes, and a clean-shaven face, with a weak, sensitive mouth. His age may have been about twenty-seven, his dress and bearing that of a gentleman. From the pocket of his light summer overcoat protruded the bundle of *indorsed* papers which proclaimed his profession.

Warrant - *A document issued by a legal or goverment office*
Indorsed - *To declare one's public approval*
Quivering – *Trembling*
Errand – *Task*
Infallible – *Perfect*
Wrung – *Squeeze*
Apprehension – *Anxiety*
Perpetrator – *Performer*

"We must use what time we have," said Holmes. "Watson, would you have the kindness to take the paper and to read the paragraph in question?"

Underneath the *vigorous* headlines which our client had quoted, I read the following suggestive narrative:

"Late last night, or early this morning, an incident occurred at Lower Norwood which points, it is feared, to a serious crime. Mr. Jonas Oldacre is a well-known resident of that suburb, where he has carried on his business as a builder for many years. Mr. Oldacre is a bachelor, fifty-two years of age, and lives in Deep Dene House, at the Sydenham end of the road of that name. He has had the reputation of being a man of *eccentric* habits, secretive, and retiring. For some years, he has practically withdrawn from the business, in which he is said to have massed considerable wealth. A small timber-yard still exists, however, at the back of the house, and last night, about twelve o'clock, an alarm was given that one of the *stacks* was on fire. The engines were soon upon the spot, but the dry wood burned with great fury, and it was impossible to arrest the *conflagration,* until the stack had been entirely consumed. Up to this point, the incident bore the appearance of an ordinary accident, but fresh indications seem to point to serious crime. Surprise was expressed at the absence of the master of the establishment from the scene of the fire, and an inquiry followed, which showed that he had disappeared from the house. An examination of his room revealed that the bed had not been slept in, that a safe which stood in it was open, that a number of important papers were scattered about the room, and finally, that there were signs of a murderous struggle, slight traces of blood being found within the room, and an oaken walking stick, which also showed stains of blood upon the handle. It is known that Mr. Jonas Oldacre had received a late visitor in his bedroom upon that night, and the stick found has been identified as the property of this person, who is a young London solicitor named John Hector McFarlane, junior partner of Graham and McFarlane, of 426 Gresham Buildings, E. C. The police believe that they have evidence in their possession which supplies a very convincing motive for the crime, and altogether it cannot be doubted that sensational developments will follow.

"Later. -- It is *rumoured* as we go to press that Mr. John Hector McFarlane has actually been arrested on the charge of the murder of Mr. Jonas Oldacre. It is at least certain that a warrant has been issued. There have been further and sinister developments in the

Vigorous – *Energetic*
Eccentric –
Unconventional
Conflagration – *Fire*
Stacks - *A pile of objects*
Rumoured – *Alleged*

investigation at Norwood. Besides the signs of a struggle in the room of the unfortunate builder it is now known that the French windows of his bedroom (which is on the ground floor) were found to be open, that there were marks as if some bulky object had been dragged across to the wood pile, and, finally, it is *asserted* that *charred* remains have been found among the charcoal ashes of the fire. The police theory is that a most sensational crime has been committed, that the victim was clubbed to death in his own bedroom, his papers *rifled*, and his dead body dragged across to the wood stack, which was then *ignited* so as to hide all traces of the crime. The conduct of the criminal investigation has been left in the experienced hands of Inspector Lestrade, of Scotland Yard, who is following up the clues with his accustomed energy and *sagacity*."

Sherlock Holmes listened with closed eyes and fingertips together to this remarkable account.

"The case has certainly some points of interest," said he, in his *languid* fashion. "May I ask, in the first place, Mr. McFarlane, how it is that you are still at liberty, since there appears to be enough evidence to justify your arrest?"

"I live at Torrington Lodge, Blackheath, with my parents, Mr. Holmes, but last night, having to do business very late with Mr. Jonas Oldacre, I stayed at an hotel in Norwood, and came to my business from there. I knew nothing of this affair until I was in the train, when I read what you have just heard. I at once saw the horrible danger of my position, and I hurried to put the case into your hands. I have no doubt that I should have been arrested either at my city office or at my home. A man followed me from the London Bridge Station, and I have no doubt -- Great heaven! What is that?"

It was a *clang* of the bell, followed instantly by heavy steps upon the stair, a moment later, our old friend Lestrade appeared in the doorway. Over his shoulder, I caught a glimpse of one or two uniformed policemen outside.

"Mr. John Hector McFarlane?" said Lestrade.

Our unfortunate client rose with a ghastly face.

"I arrest you for the wilful murder of Mr. Jonas Oldacre, of Lower Norwood."

McFarlane turned to us with a gesture of despair, and sank into his chair once more like one who is crushed.

Languid - *Slow, lazy*
Charred - *Burnt*
Rifled - *Make spiral grooves*
Assert – *Declare*
Ignite – *Catch fire*
Sagacity – *Level-headedness*
Clang – *Reverberate*

"One moment, Lestrade," said Holmes. "Half an hour more or less can make no difference to you, and the gentleman was about to give us an account of this very interesting affair, which might aid us in clearing it up."

"I think there will be no difficulty in clearing it up," said Lestrade, grimly.

"Nonetheless, with your permission, I should be much interested to hear his account."

"Well, Mr. Holmes, it is difficult for me to refuse you anything, for you have been of use to the force once or twice in the past, and we owe you a good turn at Scotland Yard," said Lestrade. "At the same time, I must remain with my prisoner, and I am bound to warn him that anything he may say will appear in evidence against him."

"I wish nothing better," said our client. "All I ask is that you should hear and recognise the absolute truth."

Lestrade looked at his watch. "I'll give you half an hour," said he.

"I must explain first," said McFarlane, "that I knew nothing of Mr. Jonas Oldacre. His name was familiar to me, for many years, ago my parents were *acquainted* with him, but they drifted apart. I was very much surprised therefore, when yesterday, about three o'clock in the afternoon, he walked into my office in the city. But I was still more astonished when he told me the object of his visit. He had in his hand several sheets of a notebook, covered with *scribbled* writing -- here they are -- and he laid them on my table.

"'Here is my will,' said he. 'I want you, Mr. McFarlane, to cast it into proper legal shape. I will sit here while you do so.'

"I set myself to copy it, and you can imagine my astonishment when I found that, with some reservations, he had left all his property to me. He was a strange little ferret-like man, with white eyelashes, and when I looked up at him, I found his keen grey eyes fixed upon me with an amused expression. I could hardly believe my own as I read the terms of the will; but he explained that he was a bachelor with hardly any living relation, that he had known my parents in his youth, and that he had always heard of me as a very deserving young man, and was assured that his money would be in worthy hands. Of course, I could only *stammer* out my thanks. The will was duly finished, signed, and witnessed by my clerk. This is it on the blue paper,

Scribbled - *Wirte or draw carelessly or hurriedly*

Stammer - *Speak with sudden pauses*

Acquainted – *Familiar*

Assure – *Promise*

and these slips, as I have explained, are the rough draft. Mr. Jonas Oldacre then informed me that there were a number of documents -- building leases, title-deeds, *mortgages*, **scrip**, and so forth -- which it was necessary that I should see and understand. He said that his mind would not be at easy until the whole thing was settled, and he begged me to come out to his house at Norwood that night, bringing the will with me, and to arrange matters. 'Remember, my boy, not one word to your parents about the affair until everything is settled. We will keep it as a little surprise for them.' He was very **insistent** upon this point, and made me promise it faithfully.

"You can imagine, Mr. Holmes, that I was not in a humour to refuse him anything that he might ask. He was my **benefactor**, and all my desire was to carry out his wishes in every particular. I sent a telegram home, therefore, to say that I had important business on hand, and that it was impossible for me to say how late I might be. Mr. Oldacre had told me that he would like me to have supper with him at nine, as he might not be home before that hour. I had some difficulty in finding his house, however, and it was nearly half-past before I reached it. I found him -- --"

"One moment!" said Holmes. "Who opened the door?"

"A middle-aged woman, who was, I suppose, his housekeeper."

"And it was she, I presume, who mentioned your name?"

"Exactly," said McFarlane.

"Pray proceed."

McFarlane wiped his damp brow, and then continued his narrative:

"I was shown by this woman into a sitting room, where a **frugal** supper was laid out. Afterwards, Mr. Jonas Oldacre led me into his bedroom, in which there stood a heavy safe. This he opened and took out a mass of documents, which we went over together. It was between eleven and twelve, when we finished. He remarked that we must not disturb the housekeeper. He showed me out through his own French window, which had been open all this time."

"Was the blind down?" asked Holmes.

"I will not be sure, but I believe that it was only half down. Yes, I remember how he pulled it up in order to swing open the window. I could not find my stick, and he said, 'Never mind, my boy, I shall see a good deal of you now, I hope, and I will keep

Scrip - *A small bag or pouch*

Insistent - *Persistent*

Mortgages - *Securities for a debt*

Insistent – *persistence*

Frugal – *Thrifty*

Supper – *Dinner*

your stick until you come back to *claim* it.' I left him there, the safe open, and the papers made up in packets upon the table. It was so late that I could not get back to Blackheath, so I spent the night at the Anerley Arms, and I knew nothing more until I read of this horrible affair in the morning."

"Anything more that you would like to ask, Mr. Holmes?" said Lestrade, whose eyebrows had gone up once or twice during this remarkable explanation.

"Not until I have been to Blackheath."

"You mean to Norwood," said Lestrade.

"Oh, yes, no doubt that is what I must have meant," said Holmes, with his *enigmatical* smile. Lestrade had learned by more experiences than he would care to acknowledge that that brain could cut through that which was *impenetrable* to him. I saw him look curiously at my companion. "I think I should like to have a word with you presently, Mr. Sherlock Holmes," said he. "Now, Mr. McFarlane, two of my constables are at the door, and there is a four-wheeler waiting." The *wretched* young man arose, and with a last *beseeching* glance at us walked from the room. The officers conducted him to the cab, but Lestrade remained.

Holmes had picked up the pages which formed the rough draft of the will, and was looking at them with the keenest interest upon his face.

"There are some points about that document, Lestrade, are there not?" said he, pushing them over. The official looked at them with a puzzled expression.

"I can read the first few lines and these in the middle of the second page, and one or two at the end. Those are as clear as print," said he, "but the writing in between is very bad, and there are three places where I cannot read it at all."

"What do you make of that?" said Holmes.

"Well, what do you make of it?"

"That it was written in a train. The good writing represents stations, the bad writing movement, and the very bad writing passing over points. A scientific expert would *pronounce* at once that this was drawn up on a suburban line, since nowhere save in the immediate *vicinity* of a great city could there be so quick a succession of points. Granting that his whole journey was occupied in drawing up the will, then the train was an express, only stopping once between Norwood and London Bridge."

Suburba - *Outskirts of a city, dull or ordinary*
Vicinity - *Surrounding a particular place ask for*
Enigmatic – *Mysterious*
Impenetrable – *Impassable*
Wretched – *Miserable*
Beseeching – *Insistent*
Pronounce – *Say*

Lestrade began to laugh.

"You are too many for me when you begin to get on your theories, Mr. Holmes," said he. "How does this bear on the case?"

"Well, it *corroborates* the young man's story to the extent that the will was drawn up by Jonas Oldacre in his journey yesterday. It is curious -- is it not? -- That a man should draw up so important a document in so *haphazard* a fashion. It suggests that he did not think it was going to be of much practical importance. If a man drew up a will which he did not intend ever to be effective, he might do it so."

"Well, he drew up his own death warrant at the same time," said Lestrade.

"Oh, you think so?"

"Don't you?"

"Well, it is quite possible, but the case is not clear to me yet."

"Not clear? Well, if that isn't clear, what could be clear? Here is a young man who learns suddenly that, if a certain older man dies, he will succeed to a fortune. What does he do? He says nothing to anyone, but he arranges that he shall go out on some pretext to see his client that night. He waits until the only other *person* in the house is in bed, and then in the *solitude* of a man's room he murders him, burns his body in the wood pile, and *departs* to a neighbouring hotel. The blood stains in the room and also on the stick are very slight. It is probable that he imagined his crime to be a bloodless one, and hoped that if the body were consumed, it would hide all traces of the method of his death -- traces which, for some reason, must have pointed to him. Is not all this obvious?"

"It strikes me, my good Lestrade, as being just a trifle too obvious," said Holmes. "You do not add imagination to your other great qualities, but if you could for one moment put yourself in the place of this young man, would you choose the very night after the will had been made to commit your crime? Would it not seem dangerous to you to make so very close a relation between the two incidents? Again, would you choose an occasion when you are known to be in the house, when a servant has let you in? And, finally, would you take the great pains to *conceal* the body, and yet leave your own stick as a sign that you were the criminal? Confess, Lestrade, that all this is very unlikely."

"As to the stick, Mr. Holmes, you know as well as I do that a criminal is often *flurried*, and does such things, which a cool man

Corroborates - *Confirms*
Trifle - *A thing of little value*
Haphazard – *Random*
Pretext – *Excuse*
Solitude – *Loneliness*
Depart – *Leave*

would avoid. He was very likely afraid to go back to the room. Give me another theory that would fit the facts."

"I could very easily give you half a dozen," said Holmes. "Here for example, is a very possible and even probable one. I make you a free present of it. The older man is showing documents which are of evident value. A passing *tramp* sees them through the window, the blind of which is only half down. Exit the solicitor. Enter the tramp! He seizes a stick, which he observes there, kills Oldacre, and departs after burning the body."

"Why should the tramp burn the body?"

"For the matter of that, why should McFarlane?"

"To hide some evidence."

"Possibly the tramp wanted to hide that any murder at all had been committed."

"And why did the tramp take nothing?"

"Because they were papers that he could not *negotiate*."

Lestrade shook his head, though it seemed to me that his manner was less absolutely *assured* than before.

"Well, Mr. Sherlock Holmes, you may look for your tramp, and while you are finding him, we will hold on to our man. The future will show which is right. Just notice this point, Mr. Holmes: that so far as we know, none of the papers were removed, and that the prisoner is the one man in the world who had no reason for removing them, since he was heir-at-law, and would come into them in any case."

My friend seemed struck by this remark.

"I don't mean to deny that the evidence is in some ways very strongly in favour of your theory," said he. "I only wish to point out that there are other theories possible. As you say, the future will decide. Good morning! I dare say that in the course of the day I shall drop in at Norwood and see how you are getting on."

When the detective departed, my friend rose and made his preparations for the day's work with the alert air of a man who has a *congenial* task before him.

"My first movement Watson," said he, as he bustled into his frockcoat, "must, as I said, be in the direction of Blackheath."

"And why not Norwood?"

"Because we have in this case one singular incident coming close to the heels of another singular incident. The police are making the mistake of concentrating their attention upon the second,

Tramp - *A vagrant or a beggar*
Negotiate - *Try to reach an agreement or compromise*
Conceal - *Hide*
Flurried - *Agitated, Nervous*
Assure – *Promise*

because it happens to be the one which is actually criminal. But it is evident to me that the logical way to approach the case is to begin by trying to throw some light upon the first incident–the curious will, so suddenly made, and to so unexpected an heir. It may do something to simplify what followed. No, my dear fellow, I don't think you can help me. There is no *prospect* of danger, or I should not dream of stirring out without you. I trust that when I see you in the evening, I will be able to report that I have been able to do something for this unfortunate youngster, who has thrown himself upon my protection."

It was late when my friend returned, and I could see, by a glance at his *haggard* and anxious face, that the high hopes with which be had started had not been fulfilled. For an hour, he droned away upon his violin, endeavouring to soothe his own *ruffled* spirits. At last, he flung down the instrument, and plunged into a detailed account of his misadventures.

"It's all going wrong, Watson -- all as wrong as it can go. I kept a bold face before Lestrade, but, upon my soul, I believe that for once, the fellow is on the right track and we are on the wrong. All my instincts are one way, and all the facts are the other, and I much fear that British juries have not yet attained that pitch of intelligence when they will give the preference to my theories over Lestrade's facts."

"Did you go to Blackheath?"

"Yes, Watson, I went there, and I found very quickly that the late *lamented* Oldacre was a pretty considerable blackguard. The father was away in search of his son. The mother was at home -- a little, fluffy, blue-eyed person, in a tremor of fear and indignation. Of course, she would not admit even the possibility of his guilt. But she would not express either surprise or regret over the fate of Oldacre. On the contrary, she spoke of him with such bitterness that she was unconsciously considerably strengthening the case of the police for, of course, if her son had heard her speak of the man in this fashion, it would *predispose* him towards hatred and violence. 'He was more like a *malignant* and cunning ape than a human being,' said she, 'and he always was, ever since he was a young man.'

"'You knew him at that time?' said I.

"'Yes, I knew him well, in fact, he was an old suitor of mine. Thank heaven that I had the sense to turn away from him and to marry a better, if poorer, man. I was engaged to him, Mr. Holmes,

Bustled - *Ruffled*
Lamented - *To express grief, Mourn*
Congenial – *Friendly*
Prospect – *View*
Drone – *Buzz*

when I heard a shocking story of how he had turned a cat loose in an *aviary*, and I was so horrified at his brutal cruelty that I would have nothing more to do with him.' She *rummaged* in a bureau, and presently she produced a photograph of a woman, shamefully defaced and *mutilated* with a knife. 'That is my own photograph,' she said. 'He sent it to me in that state, with his curse, upon my wedding morning.'

"'Well,' said I, 'at least he has forgiven you now, since he has left all his property to your son.'

"'Neither my son nor I want anything from Jonas Oldacre, dead or alive!' she cried, with a proper spirit. 'There is a God in heaven, Mr. Holmes, and that same God who has punished that wicked man will show, in His own good time, that my son's hands are guiltless of his blood.'

"Well, I tried one or two leads, but could get at nothing which would help our hypothesis, and several points which would make against it. I gave it up at last and off I went to Norwood. "This place, Deep Dene House, is a big modern villa of staring brick, standing back in its own grounds, with a laurel-clumped lawn in front of it. To the right and some distance back from the road was the timber yard which had been the scene of the fire. Here's a rough plan on a leaf of my notebook. This window on the left is the one which opens into Oldacre's room. You can look into it from the road, you see. That is about the only bit of consolation I have had today. Lestrade was not there, but his head constable did the honours. They had just found a great treasure *trove*. They had spent the morning *raking* among the ashes of the burned wood pile, and besides the *charred* organic remains they had secured several discolored metal discs. I examined them with care, and there was no doubt that they were trouser buttons. I even distinguished that one of them was marked with the name of 'Hyams,' who was Oldacres tailor. I then worked the lawn very carefully for signs and traces, but this drought has made everything as hard as iron. Nothing was to be seen save that somebody or bundle had been dragged through a low *privet* hedge which is in a line with the wood pile. All that, of course, fits in with the official theory. I crawled about the lawn with an August sun on my back, but I got up at the end of an hour no wiser than before.

"Well, after this *fiasco* I went into the bedroom and examined that also. The blood stains were very slight, mere smears and discolourations, but undoubtedly, fresh. The stick had been removed, but there also the marks were slight. There is no doubt

Trove - *A store of valuable or delightful things*
Mutilated - *Disfigured, Crippled*
Rummaged- *Searched unsystematically*
Aviary - *A large cage*
Malignant - *Infections*
Raking - *collecting*
Predisposed – *Inclined*
Brutal – *Atrocious*

about the stick belonging to our client. He admits it. Footmarks of both men could be made out on the carpet, but none of any third person, which again is a trick for the other side. They were piling up their score all the time and we were at a standstill.

"Only one little gleam of hope did I get -- and yet it amounted to nothing. I examined the contents of the safe, most of which had been taken out and left on the table. The papers had been made up into sealed envelopes, one or two of which had been opened by the police. They were not, so far as I could judge, of any great value, nor did the bank-book show that Mr. Oldacre was in such very *affluent* circumstances. But it seemed to me that all the papers were not there. There were *allusions* to some deeds—possibly the more valuable—which I could not find. This, of course, if we could definitely prove it, would turn Lestrade's argument against himself, for who would steal a thing if he knew that he would shortly inherit it?

"Finally, having drawn every other cover and picked up no scent, I tried my luck with the housekeeper. Mrs. Lexington is her name -- a little, dark, silent person, with suspicious and sidelong eyes. She could tell us something if she would -- I am convinced of it. But she was as close as wax. Yes, she had let Mr. McFarlane in at half-past nine. She wished her hand had withered before she had done so. She had gone to bed at half-past ten. Her room was at the other end of the house, and she could hear nothing of what had passed. Mr. McFarlane had left his hat, and to the best of her had been awakened by the alarm of fire. Her poor, dear master had certainly been murdered. Had he any enemies? Well, every man had enemies, but Mr. Oldacre kept himself very much to himself, and only met people in the way of business. She had seen the buttons, and was sure that they belonged to the clothes which he had worn last night. The wood pile was very dry, for it had not rained for a month. It burned like tinder, and by the time she reached the spot, nothing could be seen but flames. She and all the firemen smelled the burned flesh from inside it. She knew nothing of the papers, nor of Mr. Oldacre's private affairs.

"So, my dear Watson, there's my report of a failure. And yet --" he *clenched* his thin hands in a *paroxysm* of conviction -- "I know it's all wrong. I feel it in my bones. There is something that has not come out, and that the housekeeper knows it. There was a sort of *sulky defiance* in her eyes, which only goes with guilty knowledge. However, there's no good talking any

Fiasco – *Debacle*
Affluent – *Rich*
Privet - *A shrub of the olive family*
Allusions - *An indirect or passing reference*
Awaken – *Arouse*

more about it, Watson; but unless some lucky chance comes our way, I fear that the Norwood Disappearance Case will not figure in that chronicle of our successes which I foresee that a patient public will sooner or later have to endure."

"Surely," said I, "the man's appearance would go far with any jury?"

"That is a dangerous argument my dear Watson. You remember that terrible murderer, Bert Stevens, who wanted us to get him off in '87? Was there ever a more mild-mannered, Sunday-school young man?"

"It is true."

"Unless we succeed in establishing an alternative theory, this man is lost. You can hardly find a flaw in the case which can now be presented against him, and all further investigation has served to strengthen it. By the way, there is one curious little point about those papers which may serve us as the starting point for an inquiry. On looking over the bank-book, I found that the low state of the balance was principally due to large checks which have been made out during the last year to Mr. Cornelius. I confess that I should be interested to know who this Mr. Cornelius may be with whom a retired builder has such very large transactions. Is it possible that he has had a hand in the affair? Cornelius might be a broker, but we have found no *scrip* to correspond with these large payments. Failing any other indication, my researches must now take the direction of an inquiry at the bank for the gentleman who has cashed these checks. But I fear, my dear fellow, that our case will end *ingloriously* by Lestrade hanging our client, which will certainly be a triumph for Scotland Yard."

I do not know how far Sherlock Holmes took any sleep that night, but when I came down to breakfast, I found him pale and *harassed*, his bright eyes the brighter for the dark shadows around them. The carpet around his chair was *littered* with cigarette-ends and with the early editions of the morning papers. An open telegram lay upon the table.

"What do you think of this, Watson?" he asked, tossing it across.

It was from Norwood, and ran as follows:

Important fresh evidence to hand. McFarlane's guilt definitely established. Advise you to abandon case. Lestrade.

"This sounds serious," said I.

Sulky - *Sullen, Morose, Grouchy*
Scrip - *A small bag or pouch*
Paroxysm - *A sudden attack or violent expression*
Clench – *Compress*
Conviction – *Confidence*
Defiance – *Disobedience*
Endure – *Bear*

"It is Lestrade's little cock-a-doodle of victory," Holmes answered, with a bitter smile. "And yet it may be premature to abandon the case. After all, important fresh evidence is a two-edged thing, and may possibly cut in a very different direction to that which Lestrade imagines. Take your breakfast, Watson, and we will go out together and see what we can do. I feel as if I shall need your company and your moral support today."

My friend had no breakfast himself, for it was one of his peculiarities that in his more *intense* moments, he would permit himself no food, and I have known him presume upon his iron strength until he has fainted from pure *inanition*. "At present, I cannot spare energy and nerve force for digestion," he would say in answer to my medical *remonstrances*. I was not surprised, therefore, when this morning he left his untouched meal behind him, and started with me for Norwood. A crowd of morbid sightseers were still gathered around Deep Dene House, which was just such a suburban villa as I had pictured. Within the gates, Lestrade met us, his face flushed with victory, his manner grossly triumphant.

"Well, Mr. Holmes, have you proved us to be wrong yet? Have you found your tramp?" he cried.

"I have formed no conclusion whatever," my companion answered.

"But we formed ours yesterday, and now it proves to be correct, so you must *acknowledge* that we have been a little in front of you this time, Mr. Holmes."

"You certainly have the air of something unusual having occurred," said Holmes.

Lestrade laughed loudly.

"You don't like being beaten any more than the rest of us do," said he. "A man can't expect always to have it his own way, can he, Dr. Watson? Step this way, if you please, gentlemen, and I think I can convince you once for all that it was John McFarlane who did this crime."

He led us through the passage and out into a dark hall beyond.

"This is where young McFarlane must have come out to get his hat after the crime was done," said he. "Now look at this." With dramatic suddenness he struck a match, and by its light exposed a stain of blood upon the whitewashed wall. As he held

Littered - *Made untidy*
inanitior - *Lack of mental or spiritual vigour*
Remonstrances - *Forceful protests*
Inglorious – *Shameful*
Harass – *Annoy*
Intense – *Strong*
Morbid – *Morose*

the match nearer, I saw that it was more than a stain. It was the well-marked print of a thumb.

"Look at that with your magnifying glass, Mr. Holmes."

"Yes, I am doing so."

"You are aware that no two thumb marks are alike?"

"I have heard something of the kind."

"Well, then, will you please compare that print with this wax impression of young McFarlane's right thumb, taken by my orders this morning?"

As he held the waxen print close to the blood stain, it did not take a magnifying glass to see that the two were undoubtedly from the same thumb. It was evident to me that our unfortunate client was lost.

"That is final," said Lestrade.

"Yes, that is final," I *involuntarily* echoed.

"It is final," said Holmes.

Something in his tone caught my ear, and I turned to look at him. An extraordinary change had come over his face. It was *writhing* with inward merriment. His two eyes were shining like stars. It seemed to me that he was making desperate efforts to restrain a *convulsive* attack of laughter.

"Dear me! Dear me!" he said at last. "Well, now, who would have thought it? And how deceptive appearances may be, to be sure! Such a nice young man to look at! It is a lesson to us not to trust our own judgement, is it not, Lestrade?"

"Yes, some of us are a little too much inclined to be cock-sure, Mr. Holmes," said Lestrade. The man's insolence was maddening, but we could not resent it.

"What a *providential* thing that this young man should press his right thumb against the wall in taking his hat from the peg! Such a very natural action, too, if you come to think of it." Holmes was outwardly calm, but his whole body gave a *wriggle* of suppressed excitement as he spoke.

"By the way, Lestrade, who made this remarkable discovery?"

"It was the housekeeper, Mrs. Lexington, who drew the night constable's attention to it."

"Where was the night constable?"

Convulsive - *Fitful, Jerky*
Writhing - *Make continuous twisting*
Acknowledge – *admit*
Involuntary – *Instinctive*
Restrain – *Hold back*
Deceptive – *Misleading*

"He remained on guard in the bedroom where the crime was committed, so as to see that nothing was touched."

"But why didn't the police see this mark yesterday?"

"Well, we had no particular reason to make a careful examination of the hall. Besides, it's not in a very prominent place, as you see."

"No, no -- of course not. I suppose there is no doubt that the mark was there yesterday?"

Lestrade looked at Holmes as if he thought he was going out of his mind. I confess that I was myself surprised both at his *hilarious* manner and at his rather wild observation.

"I don't know whether you think that McFarlane came out of jail in the dead of the night in order to strengthen the evidence against himself," said Lestrade. "I leave it to any expert in the world whether that is not the mark of his thumb."

"It is unquestionably the mark of his thumb."

"There, that's enough," said Lestrade. "I am a practical man, Mr. Holmes, and when I have got my evidence, I come to my conclusions. If you have anything to say, you will find me writing my report in the sitting room."

Holmes had recovered his *equanimity*, though I still seemed to detect gleams of amusement in his expression.

"Dear me, this is a very sad development, Watson, is it not?" said he. "And yet there are singular points about it which hold out some hopes for our client."

"I am delighted to hear it," said I, heartily "I was afraid it was all up with him."

"I would hardly go so far as to say that, my dear Watson. The fact is that there is one really serious *flaw* in this evidence to which our friend attaches so much importance."

"Indeed, Holmes! What is it?"

"Only this: that I know that that mark was not there when I examined the hall yesterday. And now, Watson, let us have a little *stroll* round in the sunshine."

With a confused brain, but with a heart into which some warmth of hope was returning, I accompanied my friend in a walk around the garden. Holmes took each face of the house in turn, and examined it with great interest. He then led the way inside, and went over the whole building from basement to *attic*. Most of the rooms were unfurnished, but nonetheless Holmes

Providential - *Occurrina at a favourable time*

Wriggle - *Twist and turn with quick movements*

Hilarious - *Comical*

Insolence – *Disrespect*

Resent – *Dislike*

Prominent – *Famous*

Equanimity – *Composure*

inspected them all minutely. Finally, on the top corridor, which ran outside three *untenanted* bedrooms, he again was seized with a spasm of merriment.

"There are really some very unique features about this case, Watson," said he. "I think it is time now that we took our friend Lestrade into our confidence. He has had his little smile at our expense, and perhaps, we may do as much by him, if my reading of this problem proves to be correct. Yes, yes, I think I see how we should approach it."

The Scotland Yard inspector was still writing in the *parlour* when Holmes interrupted him.

"I understood that you were writing a report of this case," said he.

"So I am."

"Don't you think it may be a little premature? I can't help thinking that your evidence is not complete." Lestrade knew my friend too well to disregard his words. He laid down his pen and looked curiously at him.

"What do you mean, Mr. Holmes?"

"Only that there is an important witness whom you have not seen."

"Can you produce him?"

"I think I can."

"Then do so."

"I will do my best. How many constables have you?"

"There are three within call."

"Excellent!" said Holmes. "May I ask if they are all large, able-bodied men with powerful voices?" "I have no doubt they are, though I fail to see what their voices have to do with it."

"Perhaps, I can help you to see that and one or two other things as well," said Holmes. "Kindly summon your men, and I will try."

Five minutes later, three policemen had *assembled* in the hall.

"In the outhouse, you will find a considerable quantity of straw," said Holmes. "I will ask you to carry in two bundles of it. I think it will be of the greatest assistance in producing the witness whom I require. Thank you very much. I believe you have some matches in your pocket Watson. Now, Mr. Lestrade, I will ask you all to accompany me to the top landing."

Attic - *A space or room just below the roof of a building*
Parlour - *Reception or drawing room of an inn or club*
Flaw – *Fault*
Stroll – *Leisurel walk*
Untenanted – *Vacant*
Disregard – *Ignore*

As I have said, there was a broad corridor there, which ran outside three empty bedrooms. At one end of the corridor, we were all *marshalled* by Sherlock Holmes, the constables grinning, and Lestrade staring at my friend with amazement, expectation, and *derision* chasing each other across his features. Holmes stood before us with the air of a *conjurer* who is performing a trick.

"Would you kindly send one of your constables for two buckets of water? Put the straw on the floor here, free from the wall on either side. Now I think that we are all ready."

Lestrade's face had begun to grow red and angry. "I don't know whether you are playing a game with us, Mr. Sherlock Holmes," said he. "If you know anything, you can surely say it without all this *tomfoolery*."

"I assure you, my good Lestrade, that I have an excellent reason for everything that I do. You may possibly remember that you *chaffed* me a little, some hours ago, when the sun seemed on your side of the hedge, so you must not grudge me a little pomp and ceremony now. Might I ask you, Watson, to open that window, and then to put a match to the edge of the straw?"

I did so, and driven by the draught, a coil of grey smoke swirled down the corridor, while the dry straw crackled and flamed.

"Now we must see if we can find this witness for you, Lestrade. Might I ask you all to join in the cry of 'Fire!'? Now then; one, two, three -- --"

"Fire!" we all *yelled*.

"Thank you. I will trouble you once again."

"Fire!" "Just once more, gentlemen, and all together."

"Fire!" The shout must have rung over Norwood.

It had hardly died away when an amazing thing happened. A door suddenly flew open out of what appeared to be solid wall at the end of the corridor, and a little, wizened man darted out of it, like a rabbit out of its burrow.

"Capital!" said Holmes, calmly. "Watson, a bucket of water over the straw. That will do! Lestrade, allow me to present you with your principal missing witness, Mr. Jonas Oldacre."

The detective stared at the newcomer with blank amazement. The latter was blinking in the bright light of the corridor, and peering at us and at the *smouldering* fire. It was an *odious*

Marshalled - *Guided or assembled in order*
Chaffed - *Teased*
Assemble – *Collect*
Derision – *Scorn*
Conjurer – *Magician*
Tomfoolery – *Misbehaviour*

face -- crafty, vicious, malignant, with shifty, light-grey eyes and white lashes.

"What's this, then?" said Lestrade, at last. "What have you been doing all this time, eh?"

Oldacre gave an uneasy laugh, shrinking back from the furious red face of the angry detective.

"I have done no harm."

"No harm? You have done your best to get an innocent man hanged. If it wasn't for this gentleman here, I am not sure that you would not have succeeded."

The wretched creature began to *whimper*.

"I am sure, sir, it was only my practical joke."

"Oh! A joke, was it? You won't find the laugh on your side, I promise you. Take him down, and keep him in the sitting room until I come. Mr. Holmes," he continued, when they had gone, "I could not speak before the constables, but I don't mind saying, in the presence of Dr. Watson, that this is the brightest thing that you have done yet, though it is a mystery to me how you did it. You have saved an innocent man's life, and you have prevented a very grave *scandal*, which would have ruined my *reputation* in the Force."

Holmes smiled, and clapped Lestrade upon the shoulder.

"Instead of being ruined, my good sir, you will find that your reputation has been enormously enhanced. Just make a few alterations in that report which you were writing, and they will understand how hard it is to throw dust in the eyes of Inspector Lestrade."

"And you don't want your name to appear?"

"Not at all. The work is its own reward. Perhaps, I shall get the credit also at some distant day, when I permit my *zealous* historian to lay out his foolscap once more -- eh, Watson? Well, now, let us see where this rat has been *lurking*."

A lath-and-plaster partition had been run across the passage six feet from the end, with a door cunningly concealed in it. It was lit within by slits under the *eaves*. A few articles of furniture and a supply of food and water were within, together with a number of books and papers.

"There's the advantage of being a builder," said Holmes, as we came out. "He was able to fix up his own little hiding place without any *confederate* -- save, of course, that precious

Reputation - *The belief or opinion*
Yell – *Shout*
Smouldering – *Ablaze*
Odious – *Hateful*
Whimper – *Cry*
Scandal – *Disgrace*

housekeeper of his, whom I should lose no time in adding to your bag, Lestrade."

"I'll take your advice. But how did you know of this place, Mr. Holmes?"

"I made up my mind that the fellow was in hiding in the house. When I paced one corridor and found it six feet shorter than the corresponding one below, it was pretty clear where he was. I thought he had not the nerve to lie quiet before an alarm of fire. We could, of course, have gone in and taken him, but it amused me to make him reveal himself. Besides, I owed you a little mystification, Lestrade, for your *chaff* in the morning."

"Well, sir, you certainly got equal with me on that. But how in the world did you know that he was in the house at all?"

"The thumb mark, Lestrade. You said it was final; and so it was, in a very different sense. I knew it had not been there the day before. I pay a good deal of attention to matters of detail, as you may have observed, and I had examined the hall, and was sure that the wall was clear. Therefore, it had been put on during the night."

"But how?"

"Very simply. When those packets were sealed up, Jonas Oldacre got McFarlane to secure one of the seals by putting his thumb upon the soft wax. It would be done so quickly and so naturally, that I daresay the young man himself has no recollection of it. Very likely it just so happened, and Oldacre had himself no notion of the use he would put it to. *Brooding* over the case in that den of his, it suddenly struck him what absolutely damning evidence he could make against McFarlane by using that thumb mark. It was the simplest thing in the world for him to take a wax impression from the seal, to moisten it in as much blood as he could get from a pin-prick, and to put the mark upon the wall during the night, either with his own hand or with that of his housekeeper. If you examine among those documents which he took with him into his retreat, I will lay you a *wager* that you find the seal with the thumb mark upon it."

"Wonderful!" said Lestrade. "Wonderful! It's all as clear as crystal, as you put it. But what is the object of this deep *deception*, Mr. Holmes?"

It was amusing to me to see how the detective's overbearing manner had changed suddenly to that of a child asking questions of its teacher.

Confederate - *Joined by an agreement or treaty*

Brooding - *Showing deep unhappiness*

Lurking – *Loitering*

Eaves – *Attic*

"Well, I don't think that is very hard to explain. A very deep, malicious, *vindictive* person is the gentleman who is now waiting us downstairs. You know that he was once refused by McFarlane's mother? You don't! I told you that you should go to Blackheath first and Norwood afterwards. Well, this injury, as he would consider it, has *rankled* in his wicked, scheming brain, and all his life he has longed for vengeance, but never seen his chance. During the last year or two, things have gone against him -- secret *speculation*, I think -- and he finds himself in a bad way. He determines to *swindle* his creditors, and for this purpose, he pays large checks to a certain Mr. Cornelius, who is, I imagine, himself under another name. I have not traced these checks yet, but I have no doubt that they were banked under that name at some provincial town where Oldacre from time to time led a double existence. He intended to change his name altogether, draw this money, and vanish, starting life again elsewhere."

"Well, that's likely enough."

"It would strike him that in disappearing, he might throw all pursuit off his track, and at the same time have an *ample* and crushing revenge upon his old sweetheart, if he could give the impression that he had been murdered by her only child. It was a masterpiece of villainy, and he carried it out like a master. The idea of the will, which would give an obvious motive for the crime, the secret visit unknown to his own parents, the retention of the stick, the blood, and the animal remains and buttons in the wood pile, all were admirable. It was a net from which it seemed to me, a few hours ago, that there was no possible escape. But he had not that supreme gift of the artist, the knowledge of when to stop. He wished to improve that which was already perfect -- to draw the rope tighter yet around the neck of his unfortunate victim -- and so he ruined all. Let us descend, Lestrade. There are just one or two questions that I would ask him."

The malignant creature was seated in his own parlor, with a policeman upon each side of him.

"It was a joke, my good sir -- a practical joke, nothing more," he *whined* incessantly. "I assure you, sir, that I simply concealed myself in order to see the effect of my disappearance, and I am sure that you would not be so unjust as to imagine that I would have allowed any harm to befall poor young Mr. McFarlane."

Ample - *Enough*
Rankled - *Continue to be painful*
Speculation - *Guess*
Wager – *Bet*
Deception – *Dishonesty*
Vindictive – *Spiteful*
Swindle – *Cheat*
Pursuit – *Chase*
Revenge – *Vengeance*

"That's for a jury to decide," said Lestrade. "Anyhow, we shall have you on a charge of conspiracy, if not for attempted murder."

"And you'll probably find that your creditors will impound the banking account of Mr. Cornelius," said Holmes.

The little man started, and turned his malignant eyes upon my friend.

"I have to thank you for a good deal," said he. "Perhaps I'll pay my debt some day."

Holmes smiled *indulgently*.

"I fancy that, for some few years, you will find your time very fully occupied," said he. "By the way, what was it you put into the wood pile besides your old trousers? A dead dog, or rabbits, or what? You won't tell? Dear me, how very unkind of you! Well, well, I daresay that a couple of rabbits would account both for the blood and for the charred ashes. If ever you write an account, Watson, you can make rabbits serve your turn."

Food For Thought

"It is final," said Holmes. What was final according to Holmes? If the right thumb mark would not have been imprinted on the wall of the building, would Holmes be able to solve this case?

Incessantly - *Continuously*
Impound - *Seize and take legal custody*
Retention – *Preservation*
Whined – *Complained*
Conspiracy – *Plot*
Indulgent – *Generous*

An Understanding

Q. 1. "I am nearly mad Mr. Holmes, I am the unhappy John Hector Mc Farlane." Why did this man make a unceremonious entry when Holmes and Dr. Watson were chatting on their breakfast table? Why did he announce his name in this manner?

Ans. _____

_____

_____

_____

_____

Q. 2. What did Mr. Jonas Oldacre want Mc. Farlane to do for him? What was Mc. Farlane's profession?

Ans. _____

_____

_____

_____

_____

Q. 3. The first few lines of the will and the end was written very clearly as print, but the writing in between was very bad and at three places almst unreadable. Why was it so? What did Sherlock Holmes infer from this?

Ans. _____

_____

_____

_____

_____

Q. 4. Why did Holmes feel that Mc Farlane was not the murderer of Mr. Jonas Oldacre? Which are the few clues or incidents that highlight that Mr. Farlane was not the criminal?

Ans. _____

_____

_____

_____

_____

SELF-IMPROVEMENT/PERSONALITY DEVELOPMENT

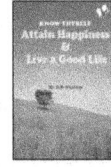

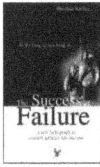

All books available at www.vspublishers.com

HINDI LITERATURE

TALES & STORIES

MUSIC (संगीत)

All Books Fully Coloured

MAGIC & FACT (जादू एवं तथ्य)

MYSTERIES (रहस्य)

ACADEMIC BOOKS

All books available at www.vspublishers.com

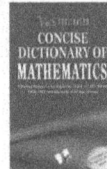

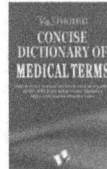

www.ingramcontent.com/pod-product-compliance
Lightning Source LLC
Chambersburg PA
CBHW070425270326
41926CB00014B/2948